VOICES

AN INFORMAL HISTORY OF 150 YEARS

FSUVOICES

AN INFORMAL HISTORY OF 150 YEARS

FSUVOICES

AN INFORMAL HISTORY OF 150 YEARS

MAXINE STERN, EDITOR

OFFICE OF THE VICE-PRESIDENT FOR UNIVERSITY RELATIONS

FLORIDA STATE UNIVERSITY

TALLAHASSEE, FLORIDA

Published 2002

Printed in the United States of America

First Edition

ISBN 1-889282-74-x

Book design by Dee Dee Celander, Celander Creative.

Printing by Boyd Brothers, Inc.

PHOTOGRAPHY

Many of the older photographs came from individuals or college yearbooks. Others
originated in one of two fine collections in Tallahassee, Florida: the Florida
Photographic Collection, Department of State, Joan Morris, Curator, or Florida State
University's Photography Archives, Strozier Library, Lucia Patrick, Director.

The FSU Photo Lab, Ryals Lee, Jr., Director, contributed many faculty and sports
photos. Ryals Lee and Bill Langford also supplied photographs from their own
collections. Ray Stanyard, in addition to the cover photo, is responsible for
others, as is Evon Streetman.

We are also grateful to the following for images on the indicated pages: Fabian
Bachrach (81); *Tallahassee Democrat* (137, 143); Le Moyne Art Foundation (109);
Robert Fichter (145); NASA (214 W. Scott); Donn Dughi (129, 132 T. D'Alemberte);
Ringling Museum of Art (177); Richard Parks (53); and Berisford Photo (215 J. King).

Every reasonable effort has been made to ensure the accuracy of the information
herein. However, neither the editor, the publisher, the Division of University Relations,
nor Florida State University is responsible for any errors or omissions which might
have occurred.

Information about FSU and its departments and programs can be found at
www.fsu.edu.

President Bernard F. Sliger (1977–1991)

Top to bottom: Tarpon Club, 1960s;
Alumni Village trailer park, 1950s;

Contents

Katherine Blood Hoffman

Alan C. Sundberg

DEDICATION

This volume is dedicated to Kitty Hoffman and Alan Sundberg,
co-chairs of the Florida State University
Sesquicentennial Campus/Community Committee.

KATHERINE BLOOD HOFFMAN (B.S., FSCW 1936)

Katherine Blood Hoffman, known as Kitty, has won the affection and respect of all who have known her. As

president of the student body of Florida State College for Women (FSCW), a member of Mortar Board and

Phi Beta Kappa, and permanent president of the class of 1936, she's cheerfully given a lifetime of service to

FSU. ¶ After earning a master's degree at Columbia University, Kitty returned to FSCW in 1940 to teach

in the Chemistry Department. In the late sixties, while serving as dean of women, she helped bring campus

dress codes up to date when she showed up to help decorate for homecoming wearing slacks. She was

greeted with, "Dean Hoffman, where is your raincoat?" and soon women students were able to wear long

pants in public. ¶ In 1978, having returned to teaching, she received the Oglesby Award for Loyalty,

Service, and Scholarship from the university, and in 1981 she was the first woman to be elected president

of the faculty senate. When she retired as a full professor in 1984, FSU dedicated the Katherine B.

Hoffman Teaching Laboratory to her as a tribute to her teaching and leadership. In 1995 Kitty and her

> ❝
>
> *But now, as the years have passed, we realize that our alma mater taught us well. We have been leaders; we have come a long way.*
>
> ❞

husband Harold endowed a scholarship for chemistry students. ¶ Kitty is a much beloved stateswoman of the Alumni Association and one of the first members of its Circle of Gold. In 1997 she was awarded the first of the university's Torch Awards for distinguished lifetime service to FSU. ¶ The following is from a welcome she gave at an alumni emeritus dinner:

We gather tonight to share precious memories as students. We recall singing of day's dying in the west, as the sun set. We wondered about the life of the spirit as we viewed the rich Maxfield Parrish sky through the tall administration building windows when darkness settled. There were classes, Thanksgiving, and "light flash" at bedtime. Some features we missed: men, football, air-conditioning, bourbon. But now, as the years have passed, we realize that our alma mater taught us well. We have been leaders; we have come a long way.

ALAN C. SUNDBERG (B.S., FSU 1955)

Alan C. Sundberg, a member of the Florida State University Board of Trustees and former chief justice of the Florida Supreme Court, died on January 26, 2002, at the age of sixty-eight. Known as a brilliant Harvard-educated attorney with a down-to-earth manner, Sundberg was credited with improving the integrity of the Supreme Court in the 1970s. ¶ He received his bachelor's degree in political science in 1955 from a newly coed Florida State University. Remaining involved with FSU after graduation, he received continuing recognition as an alumnus, including being named an ODK Grad Made Good. Sundberg practiced law for seventeen years before Governor Reubin Askew, another FSU alum, appointed him to the Florida Supreme Court in 1975. ¶ Sundberg joined Florida State as general counsel on Valentine's Day in 1997, forty-six years to the month since he matriculated at FSU. Even after he left his position at FSU in 2000, to return to private practice with the firm of Smith, Ballard & Logan, he remained involved with his alma mater. With Kitty Hoffman, he co-chaired the Sesquicentennial Committee, a group that covered everything from planning a fireworks display on the roof of Westcott to celebrating student life through 150 years. ¶ To quote Alan Sundberg: "Harvard Law School may have taught me how to think like a lawyer, but it was Florida State that taught me how to think."

> *Harvard Law School may have taught me how to think like a lawyer, but it was Florida State that taught me how to think.*

Talbot (Sandy) D'Alemberte

FOREWORD

TALBOT (SANDY) D'ALEMBERTE
PRESIDENT, FLORIDA STATE UNIVERSITY

In celebrating Florida State University's 150th birthday in 2001, let's take a moment and imagine 1851. It was only seventy-five years after the Declaration of Independence and six years after Florida decided, by a narrow vote, to become a state. Tallahassee was a remote frontier town of one square mile with only 1,500 robust, hardy, and sometimes rowdy souls—a town where men drove mules and oxen and where chickens roamed the unpaved, dusty roads. There were no gas lamps or telegraph wires. Those were the days of true wireless communication. If you wanted to talk to someone remote from you, you walked or you got on your horse. In that distant year of 1851, the legislation mandating the Seminary West of the Suwannee passed. ¶ Now let five years go by. Imagine 1856. What were the thoughts of our university's great advocate Francis Eppes—Thomas Jefferson's grandson and mayor of Tallahassee—as he rode out to the far western edge of town to survey the property and the building that had just been constructed on it? He must have dreamed about what could be accomplished here and what a university could mean to his community, his state. He must have hoped that this new institution would help bring civilization to the frontier. But he could not have imagined the achievements that Florida State University would be celebrating 150 years later. ¶ Even 100 years after the founding, during the presidency of Doak Campbell, predictions about the present time fell short. President Campbell interviewed every faculty candidate in person—something that was possible in those days. And he worked hard to hire the best and the brightest. "This is going to be a great university," he told one promising young teacher in 1951. "By the year 2000, this university will have grown so much that we'll have 10,000 students." ¶ Even a visionary like Doak Campbell could not prophesy that, by 2000, we would have more than three times that

> 66
>
> *"This is going to be a great university," Doak Campbell told one promising young teacher in 1951. "By the year 2000, this university will have grown so much that we'll have 10,000 students."*
>
> 99

many students. ¶ But even if his enrollment prediction was off the mark, it reflected a vision of greatness. If Francis Eppes and Doak Campbell could be here today—if Conradi and Murphree and our other renowned leaders could be here today—reviewing the parade of FSU's illustrious faculty, graduates, and accomplishments, I think they would be amazed. And, as I am, very, very proud. ¶ This book moves by time; it unfolds its vignettes of history in chronological order. But what if we tried to order the parade of people and events by their importance to this great university? Who would march first, second, third? We'd have to start at the beginning, of course, with the legislators who passed the law establishing the Seminary West of the Suwannee and its sister institution, now the University of Florida, and with Francis

> 66
>
> *If Francis Eppes and Doak Campbell could be here today—if Conradi and Murphree and our other renowned leaders could be here today—reviewing the parade of FSU's illustrious faculty, graduates, and accomplishments, I think they would be amazed. And, as I am, very, very proud.*
>
> 99

Eppes, who championed Tallahassee for our site. ¶ But then it gets much harder. Who was more important: the women who made the Florida State College for Women one of the greatest women's colleges in the country, or the World War II veterans who returned to enroll in the newly created Florida State University? Who were more crucial: the FSCW faculty who established one of the nation's finest liberal arts institutions and brought to this campus the state's first Phi Beta Kappa chapter, or the 49ers, the bright and dedicated professors who came after World War II and whose hard work and vision maintained the liberal arts while creating a great research university? ¶ All of them rank high. They are part of what we are today. They are part of what we will be tomorrow. ¶ Again, whose sacrifices and selfless commitment have influenced us most? Is it the young cadets who earnestly sought their mothers' permission to march to battle at Natural Bridge, or is it the many leaders and public servants—soldiers and sailors, generals, admirals, astronauts, a governor, cabinet officers, judges, and legislators—who took away from this campus a dedication to public life? ¶ Who would we have represent our most important athletic accomplishments? Our state football champions of 1905, the women of FSCW who competed in the famed Odds and Evens games, or Coach Bowden's football dynasty? ¶ Once more, they are all part of what we are today. They are part of what we'll be tomorrow. ¶ Think of those who have joined this distinguished procession in recent times: Nobel laureates; Pulitzer Prize winners; Dr. Robert Holton, the scientist who synthesized Taxol; Jack Crow and the team who successfully competed for the National High Magnetic Field Laboratory; those who have prepared the way for our new medical school; those who have led the partnership with the Ringling Museum; those who have developed distance learning. ¶ Westcott Hall was named for Justice James D. Westcott, who provided us with our first major endowment, and in that building is Ruby Diamond Auditorium, named for another great benefactor. How will we rank them with the

> **"**
> *You are part of what we are today. You are part of what we will be tomorrow. We are all the beginning of Florida State's next 150 years.*
> **"**

people like DeVoe Moore and Wiley Housewright and so many others whose generosity and hard work have brought our endowment to record levels? ¶ What, then, is the marching order of our parade? I don't think there is one. I believe the parade is a continuing procession with the generations marching forward together. ¶ And today's supporters of FSU—students, faculty, staff, and other great friends—are also a part of this procession. You are the ones who will join, arm-in-arm, as this outstanding university moves forward. ¶ You are part of what we are today. You are part of what we will be tomorrow. We are all the beginning of Florida State's next 150 years.

Jam session, 1950

A native of New York City and a graduate of the University of North Carolina, Chapel Hill,
editor Maxine Stern, like many in this book, is a Seminole by choice. Having a husband,
Jerry Stern, who taught in the English Department for many years, and a son, Bayard Stern,
who graduated from FSU, helped. As a librarian, an editor, and a staff member of the arts
festival Seven Days of Opening Nights, Stern has been a long-time FSU voice.

Preface and Acknowledgments

MAXINE STERN, EDITOR

This informal history of Florida State University, told by the people who lived it, is not intended to be an official document. The chances are good that you will know, have been taught by, or are related to some of the voices. ¶ The older ones were preserved in college publications and letters, newspapers and books. Many of the more recent ones resulted from requests for information made during Sesquicentennial events. You will find accounts of families who have sent their children to FSU over several generations, and stories from folks who didn't attend the school at all but have adopted it as their own. ¶ From the 1850s when Francis Eppes was rallying support for the Seminary West of the Suwannee, to today when graduates claim a major university as alma mater, FSU has had strong supporters. We are pleased to be able to give some of them, past and present, a chance to share their memories. For readers stimulated by this glimpse into FSU's past, we urge you to visit www.fsu.edu, where many departments and colleges present their histories. ¶ Many people deserve thanks for helping with this book. They include: Beverly Spencer and Donna McHugh, who led the way; Steve Edwards, Carmen Braswell, Diane Greer, Jennifer Brooks Agwunobi, Dawn Randle, Jim Melton, Betty Lou Joanos, Bob Celander, Betty Southard, Frank Murphy, George Riordan, Fran Conaway, Jeffery Seay, Margaret Leonard, Bayard Stern, Bill Sherrill, Frank Stephenson, Guy Moore, and Ed Augustyniak. ¶ Several wonderful writers contributed material. I'm especially grateful to Mary Ann Lindley, Diane Roberts, and Andy Lindstrom. Mike Pate, publisher of the *Tallahassee Democrat*, eased our way. ¶ Mary Lou Norwood provided invaluable assistance in researching the FSCW years. The same could be said for Robin Jeanne Sellers, author of *Femina Perfecta: The Genesis of Florida State University*. Jim Jones, as editor of *Florida State*, the alumni magazine that gradually morphed into the *Florida State Times*, provided many of the period pieces in the book. ¶ Ryals Lee, Jr., generously assembled a pictorial overview of FSU sports. He, Bill Langford, and Donn Dughi could not have been more helpful in providing photographs as well as the stories behind them. Vaughn Mancha also shared his time and memories. ¶ The book could not have been done without Ellen Ashdown and Dee Dee Celander. Bob Bruso, Jill Sandler, and Andrea and Charles Boland cheered the project on every inch of the way.

PRESIDENTS **GEORGE M. EDGAR** (1887–1892),
ALVIN F. LEWIS (1892–1897), **ALBERT A. MURPHREE** (1897–1909)

THE VISIONARIES

On January 24, 1851, the General Assembly of Florida passed an act mandating the opening of two seminaries of learning, one to be located east of the Suwannee River and the other to the west. Tallahassee, as the state capital, seemed an appropriate location for one, and Mayor Francis Eppes, a grandson of President Thomas Jefferson, worked to secure a location. ¶ In 1855, largely thanks to Eppes, the independent Florida Institute opened as a secondary school and college. It was built on "Gallows Hill," named for the spot where a woman was hanged in 1830 for killing her baby. The location's controversy, though, arose because the area was undeveloped and away from town. The Westcott Administration Building now stands where the Florida Institute once stood and is thought to be the oldest continuous site of higher education in Florida. ¶ On January 1, 1857, the Legislature passed a bill proclaiming Tallahassee the official site of the Seminary West of the Suwannee. The new school maintained the institute's liberal arts program and added four adjacent lots to the existing land, giving the campus thirteen and a half acres. The seminary did not admit women, but swift opposition soon led to the inclusion of the Leon Female Academy, which had been established in 1843 as the Misses Bates School. By 1858 the seminary was coeducational and prepared to educate the citizenry of the thirteen-year-old state.

President Albert A. Murphree

Top: Surveyors, c. 1900
Opposite: In 1855 College Hall was the first building on campus. The Westcott Administration Building now stands on the site.

In an attempt to prevent the Confederate States of America from drafting male teachers, the seminary was operated as the Florida Collegiate and Military Institute during the Civil War. Cadets attended military classes and on March 6, 1858, were called upon to fight in the Battle of Natural Bridge, just south of Tallahassee.

In spite of war and reconstruction, the Seminary West of the Suwannee took back its name and stayed open, although operating not far above the secondary level. As tourism increased in Florida in the 1880s, many visitors to the state remained, providing the tax revenue to fund the fledgling educational system. In 1880 the seminary awarded two diplomas, called licentiates of instruction. In 1885 one bachelor of arts degree was awarded, followed by seven more in 1891.

In 1887, James D. Westcott, Jr., who had attended the West Florida Seminary, died at the age of forty-eight and left a major portion of his estate to the seminary. During his lifetime he had served as a member of the state Legislature, as state attorney general and as an associate justice of the state Supreme Court. The administration building was later named for him.

The seminary board appointed George M. Edgar president in 1887. Edgar served until 1892, when Alvin F. Lewis, during whose term the student body grew from 97 to 122, took over. In 1897 Albert Alexander Murphree, a charismatic and ambitious mathematics teacher at the seminary, was appointed president.

Known for its strong liberal arts program, the school continued to prosper under Murphree's leadership and became Florida State College (FSC) in 1901. The four original colleges of FSC were Arts and Sciences, Education, Home Economics, and Music. Music instruction was important to President Murphree because he believed "the power of music increases the love for home, school and native land and thus decreases the need of jails, courts and prisons."

In 1902 Murphree hired the first doctor of philosophy, H.L. Hargrove, to teach English. The first master's degree was awarded in 1902, and the first library at the college, a room in College Hall, opened a year later. The school, with 252 students, excelled in athletics and had an intercollegiate schedule for both sexes. Florida State College fielded football teams that earned state championships in 1902, 1903, and 1905. Also in 1905 the Kappa Alpha fraternity chartered its first chapter in the state, and the senior class published an annual, the *Argo*.

The Buckman Bill of that same year, however, reorganized higher education in the state by funding only four institutions and eliminating coeducational facilities at two of those four schools. Florida State College became the Florida Female College (FFC), and the men were moved to Gainesville, taking the fraternities and football team with them.

Athletics were still very important to FFC, especially basketball. Nevertheless, in 1907 the administration prohibited public games after the current season because of the lack of dignity in the athletic costumes. The only males allowed at student games were faculty and family members of the players. Competition became scarce because other teams did not want to exclude their male friends. As a result, the students created two campus teams, the Stars and the Crescents, which gave way to the Odds and Evens—an intra-college rivalry that became a campus tradition. A girl's entering year (an odd or even number) determined her team.

The college took over the plant of the old Florida State College consisting of East Hall, West Hall, and the old Administration Building. The Administration Building stood on the present site of the Westcott fountain, while East Hall and West Hall, wooden residences, stood on the current sites of Diffenbaugh and Dodd, respectively. Of the 204 students, nearly all were high school students or students there to review the so-called "common branches" in preparation for an examination for a country teacher's certificate.

The year 1909 was a time of both beginnings and endings. The *Talisman*, a cross between a newspaper and an annual, was begun in April and printed under the auspices of the Thalian and Minerva Literary Societies. Also, the Alumnae Association was organized by Rowena Longmire. Then came another name change. The Legislature, acting on complaints about awkwardness and poor grammar, changed the name of Florida Female College to Florida State College for Women (FSCW). Finally, that same year Murphree accepted the presidency of the University of Florida. With their beloved president leaving, and a new name, it was clear that interesting times were ahead for the young women of FSCW.

Jennie Murphree,
wife of President
Albert A. Murphree

"The power of music increases the love for home, school and native land and thus decreases the need of jails, courts and prisons."

PRESIDENT ALBERT A. MURPHREE

James D. Westcott, Jr., attended the
West Florida Seminary and was a
great benefactor of the school. In
1937 FSCW named the
Administration Building in his honor.

Ruby Pearl Diamond had been a benefactor of FSU for sixty-five years by the time Ruby Diamond Auditorium was named for her in 1971. Known as Miss Ruby, she died in 1982 at the age of ninety-five.

Born on September 1, 1886, in her family's home at Park Avenue and Monroe Street, she lived in Tallahassee all of her life. She once said, "There is no place in the world like Tallahassee. I have visited all over the world and have always yearned to return." Attending school at a time of transition, her undergraduate degree was from Florida State College and her master's from Florida State College for Women.

At the time of her death, President Bernard F. Sliger, who regularly visited Miss Ruby, had this to say: "I always thought she'd live forever— sort of like my mother." He spoke for the university when he said, "It's a great loss to society and especially to Florida State."

Ruby Pearl Diamond

Opposite: Florida State College class of June 1905. This was the last coed class until Florida State University was established, and the first class to wear caps and gowns.

In 1907 the administration decided to prohibit public games after the current season ended because of the lack of dignity in the athletic costumes. The only males allowed to see student games were faculty and family members of the players.

Top: Florida State College basketball team, 1903
Bottom: West Florida Seminary baseball team, 1901

Francis Eppes VII, the son of Thomas Jefferson's youngest daughter, moved to Florida in 1928 from Virginia after the deaths of his father and grandfather. In 1841 he became intendant (mayor) of Tallahassee and served for many terms in that office.

As a public official he worked to abolish public drunkenness and to create the city's first police force. Eppes also led efforts to rebuild Tallahassee after a catastrophic fire in 1843 and in the 1850s led the Tallahassee effort to house the state-funded Seminary West of the Suwannee River. After its establishment in 1857 he spent many years on the school's board of trustees and is said to have almost single-handedly kept the school open during the Civil War. At the end of his second term in office as intendant, a grateful citizenry presented Eppes with an engraved silver pitcher.

The town's regard for Eppes's dedication led Ruth Blitch, a local historian and Florida State graduate, to lobby FSU to name a building for him. On Monday, May 1, 2000, she got her wish when the psychology building was formally named the Eppes Building. "I nearly drove them crazy," Blitch said. "They named some buildings for people who did nothing but show up on payday. I felt Francis deserved this honor."

Jim Eppes, a Tallahassee businessman and spokesman for the seven-generation family, agreed. At the time of the dedication, he said that his great-great-grandfather would have appreciated the tribute: "I think it's appropriate because Thomas Jefferson was so focused on moral and mental preparedness, and that's what he passed on to his grandson."

From the *Eppes Family History*, with thanks to Mrs. Nicholas Ware Eppes, Ruth Garrett Blitch, and Gerald Ensley

Left: West Florida Seminary cadets, 1865
Right: A cadet in uniform (photograph by Alvan S. Harper, c.1880)

The small group of Confederates huddled in their hastily built trenches, returning the fire of Union troops positioned across the narrow river. It was a scene repeated hundreds of times during the Civil War. This particular skirmish, however, was unusual in that some of the defenders were schoolboys, barely in their teens, who had been called into service earlier that day. It was March 5, 1865, and the youngsters were from the West Florida Seminary, a recently organized institution that some eighty years later would become the Florida State University.

The most crucial test for the cadets occurred in the winter of 1865, when Tallahassee was threatened by a Union advance. . . . The Federal force that had landed near St. Marks lighthouse was under the command of Brigadier General John Newton. The joint army-navy operation had originated from Union-occupied Key West, and included two black regiments, the Second and Ninety-ninth United States Colored Troops, and the Second Florida Union Cavalry.

As Newton's invaders began moving northward, Confederate officials gathered a force. Among the troops called into active service by Governor John Milton were the cadets. Milton's decision was met by apprehension by many relatives of the boys, whose ages ranged from twelve to eighteen. Nevertheless, around noon on March 5 the cadet corps, about twenty-five of the oldest boys, was assembled at the Institute and marched to the railroad station. Sue Archer, a student at the female department of the school and the sister of one of the boys, described the scene:

> *Mothers and sisters went to the station to say goodbye to them. The little fellows were full of patriotism and seemed to feel no fear. One little boy barefooted and wearing the cadets' uniform stood apart from the others, and was crying, because Captain Johnson refused to let him go, as he was the only son of a poor blind woman. Captain Johnson told him that good soldiers did not cry.*

The train carried the cadets and others south to a point on the railroad opposite Newport. From there they marched the remaining six miles to the town, joining forces with Lieutenant-Colonel George Washington Scott's Fifth Florida Cavalry Battalion. . . . The Yankees hoped to cross the St. Marks River [at Newport], enabling them to move against St. Marks and possibly Tallahassee.

Among the cadets at Newport and later at Natural Bridge was fifteen-year-old Charles L. Beard, who wrote the only known cadet account of the fighting. He recalled that the youngsters ran two at a time, into the trenches, as Union troops fired at them from across the stream. It was here that the "Baby Corps," as the boys would later be known, received their baptism of fire. One cadet, John Dubose, fell while entering the trenches. For a moment his companions thought that a bullet had found its mark but he had simply stumbled in his haste to find cover. Meanwhile, Federal forces, on the advice of local guides, decided to move upriver to the so-called Natural Bridge, a less heavily defended site.

In the late afternoon Confederate reinforcements arrived on the field and charged into the swamp. At this point the Union commander realized that, like Newport, Natural Bridge was impassable and he ordered a retreat southward. The cadets were ordered back to Newport to guard against a Union attempt to cross there. Upon reaching the town the boys received rations of corn pone, for which they had no appetite and instead used it as ammunition in a bread battle among themselves.

The cadets escorted a group of about twenty-five Union prisoners back to Tallahassee. Charles Beard sheepishly noted the enthusiastic welcome given the boys: "Many were the brave & even desperate deeds performed by the cadets according to stories current in Tallahassee upon our return—but no cadet was sufficiently damaged to need more than a good square meal to render him fit for duty." In recognition of its services, the corps was awarded a company flag during a lavish ceremony at the state capitol.

In 1957 the ROTC corps at Florida State received a battle streamer [and citation] for the cadets' actions, given "In grateful recognition of the valiant service performed by the cadets of the West Florida Seminary, lineal predecessor to the present Florida State University, who fought with distinction during the Battle of Natural Bridge, Florida, on March 6, 1865."

David Coles and Robert Bruce, *Florida State*, April 1986

Nellie Godfrey King earned a bachelor's degree in education from Florida Female College in 1906, speaking at her graduation on "Pestalozzi: His Influence on Public Education." "Miss Nellie," as she was often known, married Charles King, a teacher, principal, and superintendent of education for Jackson County. She was a prolific letter writer, beginning when she was in high school in Pensacola and continuing until 1940. Leora Pruitt King, FSCW 1942, owns the collection of Nellie Godfrey King's letters. They number over 1,000.

Tallahassee, Fla.
Nov. 19, 1905

My Dear Charlie,

. . . You just ought to be here to see all these girls. I think there are eighty-five in the dormitories, and you can imagine how much noise they make sometimes. In the whole school there are one hundred thirty-three girls, and how do you suppose we answer the roll call? Mr. Kettle, the secretary, gets up and says "roll call," and then the girls say 1—2—3 and so on to 133. I'm 49, so you can see I've been reduced to a mere number. You asked me what work we are doing. Really it is a big disappointment to us the way our work is arranged. We are reading Cicero, taking Freshman English, doing Solid Geometry, taking Elocution, voice culture, elementary physics, psychology, primary methods of teaching, model school observation, and history of education. So you see we are not getting any algebra at all. The next term we are to do "Trig," and I can't see how we are going to do it with the algebra we know, do you?

Then that English—, O My! It just makes me mad to think about it. We are in a Scott and Denny book about two years below the one we used last year, and our classmates are most of them children.

Sometimes I get so sick and tired of it all that I wish I had gone home, for I get so, so homesick sometimes.

But there, I won't write you a blue letter, so now I'm going to tell you some pleasant things. Our course in Psychology and Pedagogy is splendid. Prof. Buchholz gives us some fine lectures along those lines, and you know I'm deeply interested in those subjects. Then, too, we have a good Latin teacher—Prof. Bondurant of Chicago. He is a great friend of Mr. Cawthon, and he spoke so highly of him.

I suppose Edna has told you all about the dormitories—East and West Halls. We live in East Hall, and life here is quite pleasant but very tiresome, as I think all dormitory life is. We have electric lights and steam heat—both very convenient. The only trouble is that they turn the lights out on us every night. At a quarter to ten comes a flashlight; then at ten the lights are turned out. If we talk in our rooms after the light goes out, we get demerits. In fact we get demerits for nearly everything we do or don't do. Of course I haven't any yet but don't know when I shall have.

Edna, Lucille, and I have the dearest room. We fixed it all up last Saturday. The general color scheme is dark green and red with white for a background. It is quite pretty and cosy and since neither of us is very big, we have plenty of room. I don't think Edna has been so homesick since we came, and I know she won't get so homesick any more. . . . There goes the flashlight so I'll have to finish my letter tomorrow. . . .

You know I said I was not going to join the Literary Society this year, but over here we have to join one. There are two—the "Thalian" and "Minerva." I think I shall join the Minerva as most of the old girls belong to it. I'm not likely to join 'till I have to, as I don't feel like giving up my Saturday nights to it. . . .

Here it is tomorrow, and I've been to church. I went to the Methodist Church today with Edna and Lucille and enjoyed it very much. They have a nice church here and the people seem pleasant. Judge Parkhill made a fine address this morning—it was Rally Sunday—that charmed everybody. I met his daughter last Sunday at the Episcopal Church. She is an old Pensacola schoolmate of mine. . . .

I had a very pleasant trip over here. Met a Mr. Clark, Mr. White, and

Previous page: Cast members in an FSCW play, c.1908
Opposite: Nellie Godfrey King graduated from the Florida Female College in 1906.

Mr. Jim Thomas. Then Edith Fannin and Mary Moorehead were on the train so I had plenty of company. Lucille got on at River Junction and kept me company the rest of the way over. . . .

They won't let us write letters during the week or rather they would rather we wouldn't, so you see my writing time is rather limited. . . .

Your own little Nell

Dec. 3, 05

My Dear Charlie,

We had a very pleasant Thanksgiving, had a delightful dinner, then held a little informal tea that night, and the girls all danced. Then Mrs. Bates invited us over to her room and we had a little spread. You know we had lots of fun, all sitting around on the floor, singing songs, reciting, etc. . . . .

Yes, I've about decided to go home with Edna for Christmas, but I didn't know whether it would be all right or not, so I thought I'd ask you and Essie. She thought it would be nice, so I hope you will.

Prof. Buchholz believes in whipping sometimes. I wish you could meet him. He is a fine man but very, very peculiar.

I don't know whether I'll be better pleased over here or not, but I hope so. We went to Prof. Murphree about our work, and he is going to teach us algebra and he said he would try to change our English work.

We've just come in from picking violets and they are beautiful. . . . There are several great violet beds around the college and we are allowed to pick them whenever we choose. You know I enjoy that privilege, for you know what a crank I am about flowers. There are some beautiful ones here, too—roses, roses everywhere and other flowers.

You said you were coming over to see Edna and me before school is out. . . . All the girls said you must come and ask for all the girls you know; then they'd disappear after a while. Don't you see? For you know we're not allowed to have a young man call as a special—well, beau.

Good night, happy dreams
Nell

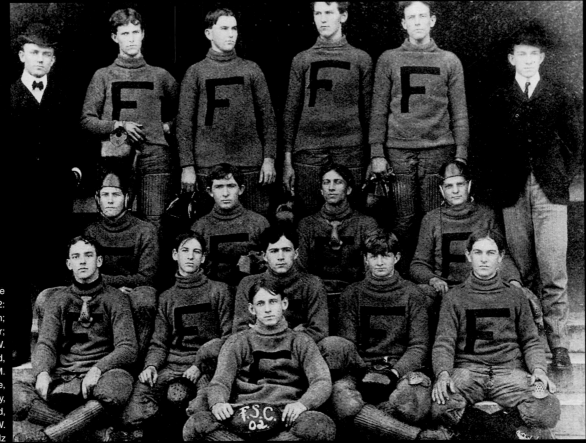

Florida State College football team, 1902: W.W. Hughes, coach; F.P. Winthrop, manager; A.B. Clark, captain; C.W. Peters, G.P. McCord, E.P. Watson, L.M. Murray, W.H. Provence, W. Mullin, W.M. Dickey, J.T. Howard, Mr. Williams, F.W. Buckholz

"If we talk in our rooms after the lights go out, we get demerits. In fact we get demerits for nearly everything we do or don't do."

NELLIE GODFREY KING

1901 graduation class, West Florida Seminary, (L to R) Bessie M. Saxon, Asa Bushnell, Lelia Jackson

In 1975 Marjory Stoneman Douglas—a popular writer on the Florida environment, an ardent defender of the Everglades, and the author of *The Everglades: River of Grass*—brought an important part of Tallahassee history back to town for safekeeping. She was afraid of the many burglaries that had taken place in her Miami neighborhood and wanted the Eppes silver pitcher kept in a safe place, the Tallahassee Historical Society.

The pitcher, given to Eppes by the early citizens of Tallahassee, is one of the few genuine reminders of that territorial period. Mrs. Douglas had bought the pitcher years earlier, mostly for safekeeping. Its engraved inscription reads, "F. Eppes Esq. Intendant of Tallahassee 1841–42. A token of regard from his fellow citizens for his untiring and successful services in the promotion of virtue and good order."

Eppes, the grandson of Thomas Jefferson, was good at cleaning up crime in the frontier town of Tallahassee. Ordinances were passed to prevent riotous and disorderly conduct, and a paid night watch, consisting of four men, was established to patrol the city from 9 p.m. to 5 a.m. An epidemic of yellow fever hit Tallahassee in the summer of 1841, taxes became high, and the city went into debt. Despite all of that the Eppes administration was reelected without opposition in 1842.

Today, the silver pitcher is mounted on a wooden base crafted from the remains of the University of Virgina's massive McGuffey Ash. The ash was planted on the grounds of the University of Virginia in 1826, shortly after its founding by Thomas Jefferson. William Holmes McGuffey, author of the famous McGuffey readers, tested his books on children beneath the branches of the great tree. It grew to 103 feet before it became diseased and was felled in 1990.

The trophy, on permanent loan from the Tallahassee Historical Society, now goes to the yearly winner of the football game between the Virginia Cavaliers and the Florida State Seminoles. The Cavaliers in 1995 were the first Atlantic Coast Conference team to defeat the Seminoles, who joined the prestigious conference in 1992.

The editor thanks Cindy Miller, Ruth Blitch and the *Tallahassee Democrat* for their assistance with this history.

Tallahassee's First Medical School

The 1868 state constitution mandated a state-run university. In 1883 a private venture to fulfil the mandate involved West Florida Seminary. State officials approved a proposal by an educator from Michigan, Dr. John Kost, to establish a school to be called Florida University. The seminary moved into one building and was known for the next two years as the Literary Department of Florida University. Kost established a college of medicine in the main seminary building, which he rented. The other divisions were to have been a college of law, a theology institute, and a polytechnic and normal (teacher training) institute. These reached varying stages of development, but the whole plan failed in little more than two years—despite the undeniable attractions of the Tallahassee locale. The first announcement of Florida University in 1883 sang the city's praises:

> *Tallahassee, the seat of the university and capital of the State, located among the hills of middle Florida, has been conceded to be one of the most lovely localities on this continent. . . . Charming Italy has no boast that middle Florida cannot match, in every element of loveliness. The climate is well nigh perfect, not too warm, not too cold at any season of the year.*
>
> *Society in Tallahassee is cultured and unconstrained by social caste. The people have been ever noted for their kind hospitality and generosity. And students that are worthy of good society will surely have it, if they wish.*

Helen Hunt, seated right, 1908

Helen Hunt was the second woman in Florida to be admitted to the practice of law. She was also the first woman to practice before the Supreme Court in Washington, D.C. She was a lawyer in Jacksonville, Florida, for forty years and her office, in the Law Exchange Building, was left intact for the use of young lawyers beginning their careers.

Mary Shuton (class of 1902)

Mary Shuton entered the Florida State College in 1899, along with her sister Fanny and brother Arthur. The two girls were members of the freshman class and Arthur was a second-year preparatory student. Mary completed her four years of college in three. When she graduated in 1902 as part of the Florida State College's first graduating class, her scholastic average was 99 1/2. She received the scholastic medal for her class each year and in her senior year was awarded the oratorical medal. After graduating from FSC, Mary received her M.D. degree from Rush Medical College at the University of Chicago. She remained in Chicago where she became a practicing physician and surgeon.

FSCW's Mary (Merry) Club. The members, all with the first name Mary, are toasting the club drinking soda pop 1910

Seal and Motto

In 1909 the legislature declared that the name Florida Female College would be changed to Florida State College for Women (FSCW). Agnes Granberry, an art student and member of the class of 1912, designed the new seal. It consisted of three torches with the words *Vires, Artes, Mores* (strength, skill, customs) on a banner and signified the mission of the college to educate students physically, mentally and morally: to create *Femina Perfecta*, the completed woman.

Robin Sellers, *Femina Perfecta: The Genesis of Florida State University,* Tallahassee: 1995

PRESIDENT **EDWARD CONRADI**

FEMINA PERFECTA

Westcott, 1915

In describing his interview with the Board of Control for the presidency of Florida State College for Women, Edward Conradi wrote: "I was questioned extensively, for they did not know me nor did I know them. The subject of my birthplace came up and they asked me, when they discovered I was from Ohio, if I got along all right with Southern children." Conradi most certainly did, as he led FSCW for more than three decades—decades that endured both World War I and the Great Depression. ¶ Yet in Conradi's tenure, the college celebrated a triumphant twenty-fifth anniversary and marked numerous academic achievements. The college gained full accreditation, and then in a single year—1924—it became a member of the Association of American Colleges, won approval from the Association of American Universities, and installed a chapter of the national honor society Phi Kappa Phi. In 1935 FSCW became home to the first chapter of Phi Beta Kappa in the state. ¶ In light of this remarkable record, one of Conradi's memories of his hiring takes on added irony. When he was finally offered the job, he was assured that FSCW would always receive support equal to that given the university in Gainesville. The promise was seldom kept; nevertheless, Conradi's leadership prevailed.

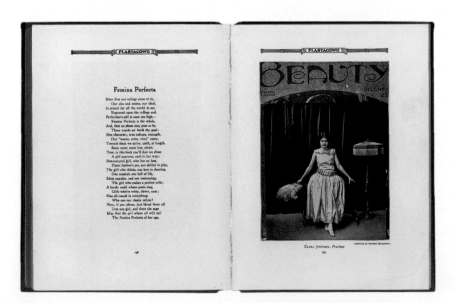

Flastacowo, 1924 yearbook

Florida State College for Women President Edward Conradi

"Dr. Conradi was a quiet man, kind but firm in his convictions. He taught two classes,
logic and ethics. It was a general belief among students that he held those classes in order to
keep in touch with the thinking of young people. To be the recipient of his slow smile and
direct gaze was equivalent to 'well done!'"

ANTOINETTE MULLIKAN VEVERKA (CLASS OF 1922)

In the early months of 1929, FSCW's credentials were so strong that it was widely referred to as "the Vassar of the South."

Lab class, 1910

Homecoming parade, 1916

1915: *Hamlet*, Dill Pickles, and a First Homecoming

In 1915, before World War I, spring at FSCW was filled with happy events as well as with the inevitable countdown to finals. A touring company performed *Hamlet* and *The Taming of the Shrew*, and the students did their version of Puccini's new *Madame Butterfly*. Clubs proliferated on the FSCW campus that spring. The AB Club took as its motto "Never do today what you can put off 'til tomorrow" and blithely expressed as its aim "to eat holes out of donuts." The Barbarians, an organization of all out-of-state students, proclaimed as its motto, "any old place I hang my hat is home, sweet home to me." The twenty-one Barbarians hailed from Georgia, Alabama, Mississippi, Kentucky, Ohio, New Mexico, Tennessee, Texas, and Missouri. Finally, there was the Dill Pickle Gang, whose fourteen members were pictured annually inside a giant dill. Emma Barrs of Jacksonville presided over this club from her office as "High Grand Pickle Eater."

In June 1915, the FSCW Alumnae Association organized a giant 10th Anniversary Jubilee for the college. In what was perhaps Florida State's first real homecoming, "old grads" joined students, faculty, and townspeople on "College Hill, with its great trees and green lawns, so enticing these warm days."

As the academic year opened in 1922, President Conradi welcomed the school's incoming freshmen: "The college is anxious and willing to serve you, but she also invites you to service." To these sentiments the *Flambeau* added: "The well-rounded student should be interested in all phases of college life, and in addition to being interested in them, should participate in them."

"All phases" included athletics and campus politics as well as academics. In the fall of 1922 basketball competition was intense as the sophomores defeated the juniors in an exciting 22–21 game to win the class championship. Then, on Thanksgiving Day, the Evens whipped the Odds 18–11. It was the third straight victory for the Evens in what had become the college's premier annual athletic event. Girls enrolling in even-numbered years joined the Evens; in odd-numbered years, the Odds.

Miss Anna Mae Tracy, a dietician who was to become one of the school's most beloved staff members, also came in 1922. She would go on to create the first meals away from home for 350 women newly arrived on the Tallahassee campus. For those students who wanted a change from Miss Tracy's tasty meals, there was "Everything Good to Eat" at the Wisteria and "the Best Club Sandwich" at the Busy Bee Cafe. While they were off campus, FSCW students might have dropped by P.W. Wilson's store to buy Jack Tar Middies at $2.95, "Dainty White Frocks" for $9.95, or "Pretty Organdy Dresses" for $1.95. Those "Jack Tar Middies" were worn daily on campus and might also come in handy on a weekend excursion to Camp Flastacowo.

Florida State, June 2, 1982

Odds basketball team, 1922

In 1907 students created two campus teams—the Odds and Evens—that became a campus tradition.
A girl's entering year (an odd or even number) determined her team.

Mayday, 1924

Antoinette (Toni) Mullikan Veverka (class of 1922)

Antoinette Veverka of West Palm Beach was a member of
Alpha Delta Pi and one of the college's leading athletes.
She had a long and successful career in journalism, writing
for the *Kiplinger Letter* and the Associated Press. Mrs.
Veverka served as editor of the *Panama City News-Herald*
and later was city editor of the *Jacksonville Journal*. In 1968
she became an editor for the *Palm Beach Daily News* and
was the longtime editor of the *Palm Beach Life Magazine*.
She died in March 1977.

As the beautiful spring term of 1930 ended, FSCW's 260 graduates were joined in final exercises by returning alumnae. From May 31 through June 4 a gala celebration hailed the twenty-fifth Jubilee of the Florida State College for Women. Alumnae president Clara Johnson Wallis participated in the dedication of a new gym. A world's growing political and economic woes seemed far away as the Jubilee class passed out of college life.

FSCW Fire Department, c. 1925–26. The Florida State College for Women formed its own fire department with Marian Watkins as fire chief. Fire captains were Dorothy Denning, Mable Poe, Mildred Bullock, Dorothy Armstrong, Sara Beredict, and Ava Leatherman.

The *Florida Flambeau* staff, 1922

As the academic year began, the faculty of 111 included 14 who have since been immortalized in bricks and mortar. Today, as in the past, students talk about Conradi, Williams, Dodd, Salley, Sandels, Opperman, Smith, Bellamy, DeGraff, Rogers, Longmire, Dorman, Montgomery, and Deviney. But seventy-five years ago, dorm conversation about those names would have used a different preposition. Instead of taking a course *in* Williams, an FSCW student would have taken a course *from* Williams.

The annual faculty-senior battle saw the faculty team, attired in a motley collection of uniforms, blast the seniors 14–6. Dr. Bellamy, faculty captain, "unearthed a uniform hinting of past glories."

In February 1927, the *Flambeau*, normally uncontroversial, editorialized on matters of grave concern to the nation and the campus. In the face of rapidly worsening relations between the United States and Nicaragua, the paper called for arbitration and opposed a war to support "Yankee Imperialism" in Latin America. The editors observed that World War I should have taught all nations a lesson about war. Closer to home, the paper pointed with alarm to recent concerts and demanded the end of "giggling, whispering, rattling programs and chewing gum."

Florida State, Spring 1977

Clockwise from top left:
1926 photographs of Nathaniel Moss
Salley, Dean, School of Education;
Mr. Elliott, gate tender; William Hudson
Rogers, English Department;
Arthur (Pi) Wiliams, Vice-President;
Rowena Longmire, English Department;
Raymond Bellamy, Social Sciences.

"One should not fail to mention Miss Longmire, an English teacher who was easily the most lovable and outgoing of all the instructors. An attractive woman, she had the peaches-and-cream complexion lauded in old novels."

ANTOINETTE MULLIKAN VEVERKA
(CLASS OF 1922)

In 1933 soon after my sophomore year began, the Great Depression settled in. My family sadly admitted that they could no longer provide money for my schooling at FSCW. At their suggestion I contacted the college business manager, John Gabriel Kellum, to see if he could suggest a solution.

Mr. Kellum asked me what my father did, and I told him that he grew citrus in Winter Haven, worth little in the current market place. Mr. Kellum directed Miss Anna Mae Tracy, head of food services, to purchase sufficient fruit from my father to feed to the students and to finance my schooling through the end of the year.

I rode the bus home, helped dad pick three truckloads of oranges, and was able to complete the academic year. There was enough money left over for me to pay for a tonsillectomy at the infirmary as well as take in a movie at the Ritz. That cost ten cents and required a chaperone if you went at night.

Can you imagine the politics and paper work that would be required to barter like that in the twenty-first century? I shall be forever grateful I was able to do it. Rumor had it that another student "made it" in school during that time on sweet potatoes, although I've never been able to confirm it.

Ella Scoble Opperman was dean of the School of Music from 1911 to 1944. A story relates that her birth was announced in the Harrison, Ohio, weekly paper as follows: "The Oppermans have bought a brand new family organ." Perhaps the comment was prophetic for a child who later became a master of organ music.

Rebecca King Spooner

Excerpts from a letter she wrote to her mother, Nellie Godfrey King, in April 1933. Rebecca's father has just died, and she has returned to FSCW. Her brothers, Bryan and Godfrey, also lived and worked in Tallahassee.

Dearest Mama,

Another week is almost gone. Just four more weeks until school is all over for this time. It just doesn't seem possible.

The legislators were entertained at an informal sort of dinner in the college dining room tonight. The Marianna girls all sat at one table with Mr. Wynn and Mr. Lewis. Mr. Dickson was entertained at the other Jackson County table. . . . Mr. Dickson is very plain, but is a lot of fun. His tallness seemed to attract quite a bit of attention from the other girls.

We are going on our all day bird trip this Saturday. We are going to a pond about five miles out from Monticello. Bryan is letting me have his car, and three more cars are going so you see we have quite a crowd. Miss Deviney does things in a big way. We are to have a rather elaborate lunch, I think. There are about four faculty members besides Miss Deviney going. One girl said, "too many uppity-ups for me to have a good time."

Good night with just loads of love to you, dear Mama.

1929: Silly Singing, Cutting Classes, and Helen Keller

In spring 1929, as the depression began to cast its shadow, the *Flambeau* struck out at a number of less-weighty problems. A March editorial attacked "Saturday night singing in the dining room, a custom begun only four weeks ago." The writer found the custom "nothing short of ridiculous. Any regular dining room singing other than the blessing takes on the appearance of boarding schools or little one-horse prep schools." The *Flambeau* also tackled a more controversial subject—college no-cut policy. Supporting a liberalized policy, the editorial asked, "Are we still children or are we college women?"

With the blind date just making its appearance as a social phenomenon, the 1929 *Flastacowo* annual offered this exchange between two students:

"What—going out on a blind date?"

"Yeah; Columbus took a chance, you know."

"Well, I hope you don't discover anything as old as America!"

More serious springtime business was the appearance of two campus speakers. In May famed Southern sociologist Howard Odum talked to the students. One month earlier Helen Keller delivered an address on world peace and brotherhood. "You can do anything you wish if you stick to it," proclaimed the courageous Miss Keller. It was good advice to graduates soon to find themselves the younger generation of their nation's most crippling depression.

Florida State, Summer 1977

1930: Date Parlors, the Talkies, and "Spondulix!"

FSCW students faced the new decade with a relaxation of the rigid rules that had confined their older sisters in the twenties. Date parlors now existed where students might sit with male friends. Bridge, banned but played clandestinely in the past, was now legal. Restrictions, designed to keep students away from downtown Tallahassee on Saturday, had also been removed. Tallahassee's Daffin Theatre offered "100% all-talking movies": Helen Morgan in *Applause*, Marilyn Miller in *Sally*, and Episode No. 3 of *Tarzan the Tiger*.

As spring approached so did some new fads and fashions. Bicycling was the rage with groups of college women wheeling in all directions. On March 14 a *Flambeau* headline proclaimed: "Spring Fever Hits Campus. Girls Find Many Diversions." Among these were hiking, nature study, gardening, and making dresses. Vivid colors were popular as "wild Irish green, clear marine blue, corn yellow, and American Beauty red" adorned the young women of Florida State.

Each campus generation had its own slang, and this one was no different. "Spondulix" was the word for extreme disaster as in "I'm broke, haven't a spondulix to my name." "She's a bear" or "she's the berries" was the highest note of praise awarded, and "cat's pajamas" and "cat's whiskers" were still alive as superlatives. A smart-looking coed was "slick" or "nouella" or was called a "line shooting individual."

In early March the junior-senior prom brought Governor Doyle Carlton and 260 other guests to the FSCW campus, most coming from Gainesville. Music was provided by the Banzai Currie Orchestra, the most popular ensemble on the University of Florida campus.

Florida State, Winter 1980

Anna Forbes Liddell, known as "Forbes," professor emerita of philosophy, died in 1979. She was remembered at the time for standing four feet ten and one-half inches tall, for having gleeful brown eyes, an engaging voice, and for teaching with such clarity and wit that many a twenty-year-old in her class wondered how he or she came to be less youthful than the professor.

Daisy Flory, in speaking of her former professor and longtime friend, said "One can hardly deny that many FSCW customs—light flash at 10:30 p.m., signing out and in for any kind of trip off campus, rigid dress and personal conduct codes, etc.—might have had disastrous and narrowing effects but for the free and fiery spirit of Forbes Liddell and other strong and liberated women who came to the faculty and stayed because Forbes was here."

Dr. Liddell came to FSCW in 1926 as part of an effort to upgrade the faculty. She had a Ph.D. from the University of North Carolina, the first woman to take the examination for the doctorate and the first student to receive the doctor's degree in philosophy at North Carolina. She was professor of philosophy at FSCW and FSU for thirty-six years and was head of the Department of Philosophy for most of that time. She was also responsible for setting up the program in humanities at FSU.

When Dr. Liddell was named distinguished professor of the year in 1959, Dr. Marian Irish said of her, "She has the rare ability to communicate the most abstract philosophical ideas in such a way that students can make them their own."

At sixteen, and about to make her first trip to Paris, Forbes was warned by her father that French men would ply her with heady French wines which might have an effect on her. He advised her, "You had better avoid the wine and stick to bourbon to which you're accustomed."

The ghost of her father seemed to be present years later when, at the age of eighty-one, she appeared before the committee that was considering whether to send the Equal Rights Amendment to the floor of the Florida House of Representatives for a vote. The meeting was held in the House Chamber and the galleries were packed with both pro-ERA and anti-ERA forces. When Liddell was wheeled to the microphone and got out of the wheelchair, there seemed to be a general fear that she might fall or be overcome by excitement. She began by saying that she found the arguments of the opposition very interesting, that in fact she had heard the same arguments made against women's suffrage. In 1916 she had marched up Fifth Avenue in a women's rights parade, and was an usher at the suffrage rally at the Metropolitan Opera when President Theodore Roosevelt spoke.

Forbes asked the men to think of their daughters and said, "I've never seen a father who didn't think his daughter was every bit the equal, or maybe even a bit superior, to another man's sons." She said the opposition was wrong to imply that every woman had a sweet, wonderful, protective husband. "I'm an old maid, I've never had a husband—not mine or anybody else's," she declared. And in describing her long career as writer, professor, and department head, she said, "In every position that I have held, I was preceded by a man, and I was followed by a man, so I guess you could say that I do a man's work."

Dr. Liddell was a parishioner at the Episcopal Student Center, across the street from her house. She gave George Bedell grades on his sermons when he was rector there. When she sat in the pew, her feet were well above the floor. When fellow parishioner Paul Piccard knelt, he was taller than Anna Forbes was standing. Looking down at her from his kneeling position he once said, "Kneeling or standing, I'll never be as tall as you, Anna Forbes Liddell." When she lost the tip off her walking cane, she told Chaplain Lex Mathews that she was afraid she might slip. He put a champagne cork on the end of her cane, and she seemed in no danger of slipping the day he found her swinging her cane through the strings and stakes he had stretched across the lawn to keep students from making paths through the yard. "We're trying to let people in the church, not keep them out," she said as she reopened her favorite path. Mathews said of her, "There was a lot of woman-ness about her. She was so small, she wasn't the kind of person you think of as being sexy, but there was a sexuality about her. It's like she was a certain kind of woman when she was young and she stayed the same from age twenty until she died."

She loved to go to the theater, and her memories of plays and

"In every position that I have held, I was preceded by a man, and I was followed by a man,
so I guess you could say that I do a man's work."

ANNA FORBES LIDDELL

concerts from the first half of the century enriched the knowledge of students who saw more modern productions with her. When she attended *The Importance of Being Earnest* in 1978, at FSU, she recounted the version of it she had seen in London in 1925. That production, staged using the colors allegedly preferred by Oscar Wilde—sets and costumes in black and white with just a few touches of red and purple—evoked the *fin-de-siècle* irony of the play.

Watching the excellent, comparatively straightforward performance by their contemporaries, the young women gained a perspective on their own era and on the life of the play. When asked if she had seen Martha Graham's 1932 concert at FSCW, Liddell said, "Oh my yes. She was here several times. It was very nice."

Linda Harkey, *Florida State*, Spring 1980

Jennie Murphree Hall, Florida State College for Women, Tallahassee, Florida.

Main Entrance and Administration Building, Florida State College for Women, Tallahassee, Fla. 11

T.26 BROWARD HALL, FLORIDA STATE COLLEGE FOR WOMEN, TALLAHASSEE, FLA.

1934: Phi Beta Kappa, Claude Pepper, and Radio Fees

The most significant news at Florida State College for Women as 1934 rolled in was that the college had been awarded the first Phi Beta Kappa chapter in the state. The prestigious national honorary cited FSCW's "high standards" in welcoming it to membership.

On the style horizon in '34 were "bangs," like those worn by Katherine Hepburn in *Little Women*. Naturalness as opposed to glamour was also "in." Best-selling magazines at FSCW were *Colliers*, *Liberty*, *Saturday Evening Post*, and *Time* (in that order).

When asked how they spent their "nickels," the young women listed movies, beauty, food, laundry, stamps, and cigarettes, with food clearly in the lead. Coeds spent money at the Sweet Shop, the Goody Shop, Spic and Span, Bennett's College Inn Pharmacy, the Three Torches, and the Dutch Kitchen.

One sign of the times, in spite of FDR's theme of "Happy Days Are Here Again," was the continuous transfer of students to FSCW. In a time when undergraduate transfers were relatively rare, the depression led to an increase. Florida women who had gone north to Wellesley and Boston University came back to less expensive Florida State College for Women that mid-year break.

The most popular lecturer to appear at FSCW in '34 was a Floridian on his way up in the political arena. On March 23 a speech on "Women in Politics" was delivered by a "prominent young Florida attorney" named Claude Pepper.

The liberalization of social rules at the college continued. Weekend privileges were expanded, and the use of chaperones by the college administration, long opposed by the students, declined still further. Another change brought permission to play radios during "music hours" if a fee had been paid to cover the expense of the electricity used by the newfangled and increasingly popular means of communication.

Florida State, Summer 1984

A driving force for modern dance at FSCW and FSU was Nellie-Bond Dickinson, professor and chair of dance from 1935 to 1963. Dickinson (known to many as Bondie), brought the dance program, which was then within the physical education department, to a new level with her own choreography and performance and by twice bringing Martha Graham to campus. Dickinson studied with Graham in New York, an experience that she has said was life-changing.

Over nearly three decades, Dickinson herself marked many lives, and in 1998 at the spring reunion of FSU's Emeritus Alumni Society, she was honored with a tribute concert, a reception, and a contribution from supporters and friends of more than $1,000 for the Heritage Tower landmark. In 2002, with a generous gift of $100,000, Dickinson established an endowed fund allowing Department of Dance faculty and students to study with professional companies. Dickinson took her bachelor's degree from Woman's College, University of North Carolina at Greensboro, her master's from Teacher's College, Columbia University, and on leaving Florida State taught at Marymount College of Virginia.

Beth Walton Moor graduated from FSCW, she said, with the class of 1919 even though she finished a year before that. It was the class she went in with and would remain *her* year.

When the Friends of the FSU Library was formed, Moor was a charter member and its first president. She was also a charter member of the Board of Trustees of the FSU Foundation.

When writers Cornelia Otis Skinner and Marjorie Kinnan Rawlings came to speak at the school, Moor entertained them. Her most famous guest was Eleanor Roosevelt, who came to speak at FSCW in 1940. "It was a very hectic time," Moor said. "It rained hard all day, and secret service men swarmed around the campus and around our home."

On June 3, 1967, Beth Moor Day was held at FSU, with three Florida governors present: Millard Caldwell, Spessard Holland, and Leroy Collins. Four hundred people attended a banquet in her honor and heard President John Champion say: "When I think of Beth Moor, I think of Florida State University and her love for her alma mater. I think of her immediate response to any call from us for help or advice."

Bettie Clifton Moor Bedell, Daughter of Beth Moor

Florida State College for Women was a part of the lives of everyone in our family for as far back as I can remember. You can just imagine growing up with a dynamite mother who was passionate about her community and particular interests, among which FSCW was at or near the top of the list.

I vividly remember going with Mother to see Dr. Conradi when he was president. I don't know the reason for the visit, but I was very impressed by the house the college provided for him. It was a large frame house on the north side of College Avenue about three or four blocks from the campus. Thinking back on it, I'm sure it was probably cold in the winter. I believe the rooms were very large with windows which were not insulated! Drafty would be a good description.

Activities on the campus I remember most were swimming exhibitions or competitions in Montgomery Gym. The Odds and the Evens had competitions of all sorts, but the ones I liked the best were swimming. I can still remember the strong odor of chlorine when you entered the gym. Also the Tarpon Club had exhibitions of synchronized swimming. It was my ambition to be good enough to be selected to be a member of the Tarpon Club.

I remember when Eleanor Roosevelt came to Tallahassee to give a speech at the college. She had dinner at our house and was very gracious about posing for many pictures with our family and our numerous relatives. I don't remember being as impressed by having Mrs. Roosevelt in our home as I was when I met Tarzan at Wakulla Springs.

One of the real joys of our daily life was when the man driving a mule pulling a wagon came through the neighborhood selling fresh produce. It seems to me he came when we were eating in the breakfast room. Other times Mother went to the curb market which was downtown on East Gaines Street. The ladies would go very early in the morning and bring live chickens and fresh vegetables back for the cook to prepare.

Another memory from early childhood was the coming of public transportation. I think it must have been a weekend when we gathered the neighborhood children to ride unchaperoned on the bus for the complete round trip. The fare was just one nickel for the whole trip, which we all thought was a bargain—best money spent for baby sitting. The route was all the way to the train station and back.

I also remember Cornelia Otis Skinner's visit, although she did not come to the house. Mother went to the Floridan Hotel to pick her up and take her to the college for her talk. My brother and I went in to get her, and I felt very special being in the elevator with her. She was very entertaining, especially when she gave a monologue about homework. She was a very attractive woman, and she wore a lovely long evening dress.

Eleanor Roosevelt visited FSCW in 1940.
(L to R) Beth Moor, unidentified woman,
Eleanor Roosevelt, President Edward Conradi

"I remember when Eleanor Roosevelt came to Tallahassee to give a speech at the college. She had dinner at our house and was very gracious about posing for many pictures with our family and our numerous relatives. I don't remember being as impressed by having Mrs. Roosevelt in our home as I was when I met Tarzan at Wakulla Springs."

BETTIE CLIFTON MOOR BEDELL

In 1918 the young sociologist Raymond F. Bellamy taught a variety of courses in sociology, economics, history, and political science at the Florida State College for Women. In 1925 he offered the first year-long course in anthropology, thought to be "probably the first such course south of Johns Hopkins University."

Stimulated by this course and his conviction that "whenever any person studies another group he never quite understands them because he's seeing it from the outside," in 1925 Bellamy wrote a tongue-in-cheek article which was published in 1927 by the *Methodist Quarterly Review*. Titled "M'Lamblo's Study of American Religion," Bellamy wanted to show how easy it is to make mistakes when studying another religion from the outside.

The observer in his satire is M'Lamblo, an educated Polynesian who spent five years in the United States studying religion. M'Lamblo reports on the many, many deities in America, among them Santa Claus, who has his special day, whose effigy is widely displayed, and in whose worship Americans spend all their worldly goods—returning after the Santa Claus season to a state of poverty. There is also the dog whose worship is reflected in such phrases as "doggone" and whose flesh is symbolically eaten in the "symbolical hot dog." He also points out to his Polynesian audience that "dog" spelled backward is "god." Cows, M'Lamblo reported, were not holy, though a woman used the expression "holy cow" quite frequently and there may have been a bovine deity named Bull Durham. Animism is very prominent (though universally denied) as men talk to their golf balls with great earnestness. M'Lamblo explains that there still are traces of a crude theory of descent from totemic ancestral animals: "There are still many who cling to the old notions and insist on literally interpreting the traditional beliefs that they are descended from animals, particularly that apes were their ancestors. But there is a very strong fight against this conservatism by a group of daring progressives who insist that this is all a myth, and preach that man has no animals among his ancestors." In conclusion the educated Polynesian admitted to his audience that he could be as badly mistaken in his observations on American religion as some of them might have been "who have studied the religion of us Polynesians."

These were the days of the Scopes trial, and this kind of talk was not acceptable. A formidable group of influential men, including Governor Syd Catts, opposed Bellamy. The Florida Purity League, with the avowed aim of ridding the libraries of offensive material, was formed. Catts was up for reelection and vowed that if elected, he would appoint a new board of control every week, if necessary, but Bellamy would go.

The group insisted that President Conradi fire Bellamy since there was no place in the state educational system for a pro-German, a Bolshevik, an atheist, a teacher of evolution and of free love, and in addition a Damnyankee. Conradi refused but advised Bellamy not to rock the boat. Catts lost the election to Doyle E. Carlton, Sr., and education in Florida became more enlightened. The course that Bellamy started continued, and Bellamy himself retained his interest and involvement in anthropology.

Brian M. DuToit, *Florida Journal of Anthropology*, special publication, 1986

Raymond F. Bellamy

Opposite: On October 31, 1935, President Edward Conradi confers an honorary degree on Ruth Bryan Owen, the first woman from Florida to serve in Congress. She was the daughter of William Jennings Bryan.

It was Dr. Edward Conradi's last fall as president of FSCW. On October 1, Dr. Doak S. Campbell would arrive to become the school's third president. It was also the last peacetime fall for a while.

In mid-October the changing nature of American life was brought home graphically, and pleasantly, to FSCW. Troops from the 31st Division came through Tallahassee on their way to Camp Blanding from maneuvers in Louisiana, staying for four days. The Sweet Shop and dorm entrances swarmed with khaki-clad men and college women. "Refreshing, very," commented the *Flambeau* and added, "At 10:30 every one of the four nights, the girls scuttled back to their dorms. Some sported army pins, others fatigue caps. Then it was all over."

A new president and a hurricane arrived in October. Doak Campbell announced that he didn't plan major changes. The hurricane was not so sensible. A 75 mile-per-hour wind ripped through campus uprooting and splintering trees and blowing down wires. Fortunately, no one was hurt and buildings escaped major damage.

The campus population in 1941 numbered 1,987.

Just after Thanksgiving FSCW students, participating in the Bundles for Britain program, shipped two boxes of goods to Churchill's valiant island. On December 8 they heard FDR describe "a day that will live in infamy," and one day later they assembled to hear President Campbell, who began his presidency in October 1941. He urged them to remain calm, pointing out that "we should take lessons from our British friends." Campbell told the convocation, "You must study hard because it is more than ever up to college women to keep alive American culture and idealism."

Florida State, 1979

Margaret Grace Fishler Fleet (class of 1939)

I graduated from the FSCW in 1939 with a bachelor of arts degree. My aunt, Jennie Mendelson, was the sponsor of Delta Phi Epsilon sorority while I was the president of the Panhellenic organization.

The Mendelsons' two sons, Sidney and Harold Mendelson, still reside in Tallahassee. Harold's wife, Lillian (Fleet) Mendelson, graduated from FSCW in 1930. She is a sister to my husband, Joel Fleet, M.D. Sidney's dear departed wife, Rosalind Mendelson, also attended FSCW.

Robert Frost visits campus in 1940.

"I want poets to be declared equal, I guess, to—what shall I say, scientists?
No, big businessmen. I want poets declared equal to big businessmen."

QUOTED IN HELEN MUIR, *FROST IN FLORIDA: A MEMOIR,* **VALIANT PRESS, 1995.**

PRESIDENT **DOAK S. CAMPBELL**

WAR AND MEN

President Doak S. Campbell

In 1941 the Japanese attacked Pearl Harbor, and Florida State College for Women was moved to action. Air-raid drills were mandatory for students as well as faculty, and in 1942, "Radio Code Practice" and "Defense Mechanics" were added to the course schedule. ¶ Thousands of returning World War II veterans intent on using their G.I. Bill education benefits caused the Legislature to return FSCW to coeducational status in 1947. Another, and final, name change was official: Florida State University. Departments of education, home economics, and music already existed in the College of Arts and Sciences. Soon library science, social welfare, business, and nursing were added. ¶ Campus life too reflected the changes. With athletics extended, students adopted the Florida Seminole Indians as their teams' symbol. The unique Flying High Circus was created, an attempt to provide an activity that both men and women could enjoy together. ¶ President Doak S. Campbell led the way through the transition years, immediately emphasizing the sciences to balance the existing strengths in the liberal arts. Achievements were fast and impressive as hundreds of new faculty arrived. Winthrop Niles Kellogg, who joined the FSU Psychology Department in 1950, provides just one example. He was the first person to raise an ape in a human environment and later discovered that porpoises use echolocation to navigate.

Opposite: Victory Club, 1942

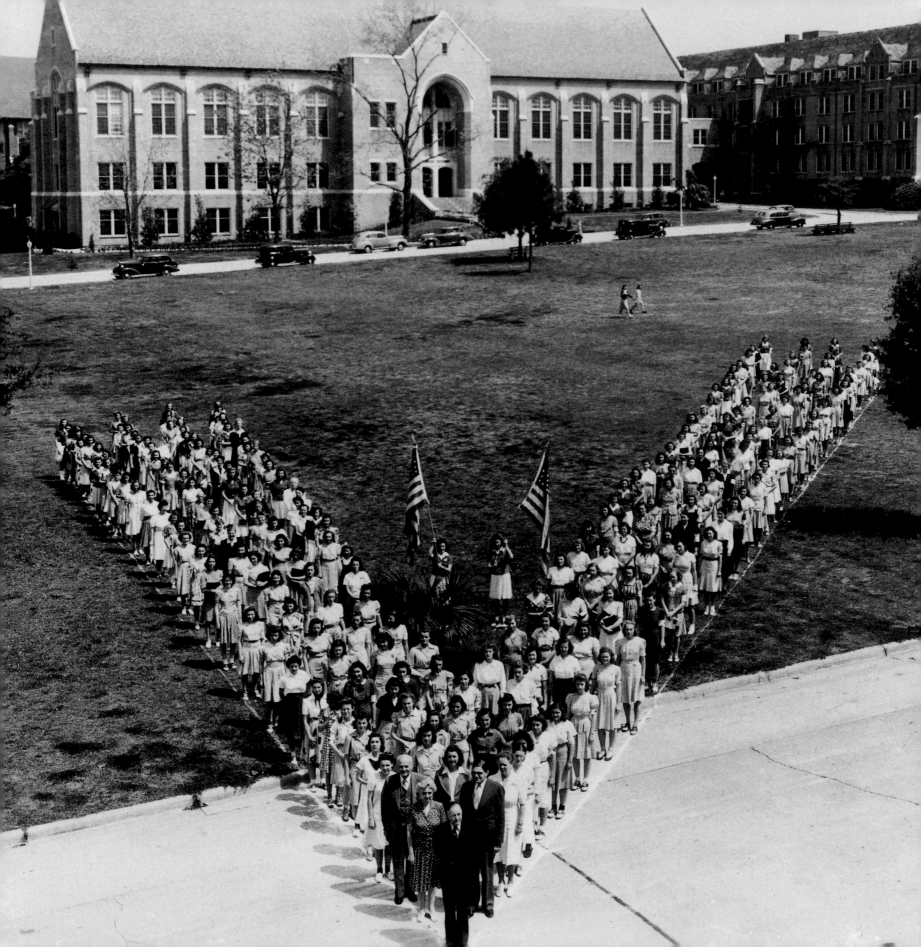

Anne Gaylord Richardson (class of 1942)

These excerpts are from a 1941 letter Anne Gaylord Richardson wrote to her aunts in Ohio. Anne majored in English literature and journalism, earning a bachelor of arts degree in 1942. While in school she wrote for the FSCW magazine, the Distaff, *and for the college newspaper, the* Flambeau.

The soldiers are going through here on their way to Blanding from war maneuvers, and the town is simply swamped with them. The drugstores uptown are a veritable sea of khaki. The campus is more than dotted with uniforms. And all in all I don't see how Tallahassee has survived having so many males all at once.

That has added somewhat of a variety to our daily life, but mother nature really did the job up brown. Night before last it began to rain. Then about five a.m. it struck. Of course yours truly was sleeping then, but when I did waken the wind was howling plenty.

At quarter of seven the electricity went off. Breakfast was somewhat of a madhouse and after we began wondering about classes. Every telephone in the building was busy, girls calling Dean Dorman, the registrar, and the new president to find out whether or not there were going to be classes. Each dormitory had a different version. Dean Dorman said definitely yes, the president said it was impossible for us to go, certain teachers said their classes would or would not meet. Meanwhile the wind blew on and the rain poured in.

In town chimneys are down, the huge plate front of one of the drugstores is gone, no electricity. The ice plant is furnishing the college and commercial places from their delco, but everyone else is in darkness. The only way we can get in touch with the outside is through the air base. Saint Marks, on the gulf, was evacuated and Carrabelle is supposed to have had a tidal wave.

I must make my bed and clean this room up somewhat. After all, the hurricane didn't come in.

Opposite: Looking east from Wescott,
FSCW choral group, 1940

Leora Pruitt King (class of 1942)

One warm Sunday afternoon in early December 1941, my roommate Anne Gaylord and I were studying in our courtyard-facing room in Landis Hall. We kept hearing the very loud sound of a radio blaring. I remember yelling out the window to "turn your radio down!" Of course it did no good. Just before supper time my good friend, Sadie Lentz, knocked on our door and told us that the Japanese had attacked Pearl Harbor. My response was "Where is Pearl Harbor?"

We went to the dining hall for supper, all of us feeling shocked that we were at war and wondering what next. At first there was the usual buzz from the two thousand of us, then suddenly total silence in that beautiful cathedral-like room, followed by the usual buzz, then silence again. The periods of silence gave me such an eerie feeling.

The next day President Roosevelt addressed a joint session of Congress making his famous "Day of Infamy" speech. I don't remember if Anne and I cut classes or not, but I know we heard his speech on the radio in our room. We simply were not going to miss that.

Another time that I was impressed by the joint reaction of the students was on the occasion when Eleanor Roosevelt came to speak to us. We were all dressed in our best and gathered in the auditorium of the Westcott building. When Mrs. Roosevelt entered from the rear of the auditorium to walk down the aisle to the stage, there was absolute unbroken silence. From two thousand girls it was a show of the deep respect we felt. As for me, I could almost feel her presence; I suppose the others did also.

During the war years there were various extracurricular training courses offered. One I took was auto mechanics. Among other things, we learned to adjust carburetors and change spark plugs and flat tires. It was knowledge that would come in handy when driving alone. Once, coming down a dirt mountain road in Venezuela, I had two flat tires in one afternoon. At that time I really appreciated Florida State's training.

The day I graduated I received a telegram saying, "You know if there were any way I could be there to see you graduate, I would be there. Dad." It was from an embarkation point in New Jersey; my father was on his way to England as the Communications Officer for the 8th Air Force.

Two days later I was at work at the Eglin Air Force Proving Ground in the Florida panhandle.

"We went to the dining hall for supper, all of us feeling shocked that we were at war and wondering what next. At first there was the usual buzz from the two thousand of us, then suddenly total silence in that beautiful cathedral-like room, followed by the usual buzz, then silence again. The periods of silence gave me such an eerie feeling."

LEORA PRUITT KING (CLASS OF 1942) THE EVENING OF THE ATTACK ON PEARL HARBOR

FSCW students garden for the war effort.

Although the college on the hill in Tallahassee seemed a long way from the war that held the world in its grips, a close look in the first months of 1943 revealed that the conflict had come to FSCW. "Your Army has scores of jobs for alert college women—jobs vital to the war," read an ad for the AWACS in the *Flambeau*. Every issue of the paper had its large ad for War Bonds and Stamps.

Even the curriculum reflected the national crisis. FSCW offered a military mapmaking course as well as a vegetable gardening course. In February, President Doak S. Campbell went to Washington to an AAUW meeting whose subject was "coordinating the resources of women's colleges."

That winter, notice reached all FSCW students that "Ration Book No. 2" would be issued. When each student received her book she had to declare all coffee on hand. No one was permitted more than one pound.

That spring the college's calendar was altered by wartime shortages. Spring holidays, March 27–April 1, were canceled because of transportation problems. Then, commencement was moved forward from May 31 to May 27. A convocation of concerned young women listened in March to Florida Senator Claude Pepper speak on "Phases of the World Situation."

One of the most interesting wartime problems in Tallahassee was addressed in a *Flambeau* editorial on February 5: "We are still faced with our 'Saturday night problem.' Soldiers continue to pour into Tallahassee while we students stay on campus in our effort to cooperate with town and college requests. But recreational facilities still do not fill community needs and Saturday nights continue to be the 'free' nights on campus."

While World War II made its impact on the Tallahassee campus, life in many ways went on as usual for the college's 1,600 students. Sorority initiations, sorority banquets and the spring's prom were held as usual.

A survey was taken that spring in an attempt to discover the favorite spare-time activities of FSCW students. First on the list was reading; second was letter writing, followed by "bull sessions," hiking, and sports.

Not making the top of the list, but very popular nevertheless, was pop music and the movies. In February the campus listened to Glenn Miller's "Jukebox Saturday Night," Benny Goodman's "Why Don't You Do Right?," Dinah Shore's "I Can't Give You Anything but Love Baby," and the great Duke Ellington number "Don't Get Round Much Anymore." At the Florida Theatre students could take in a strange double feature: *Bambi* and *Commandoes Strike at Dawn*.

Florida State, **June 1982**

Milton W. Carothers

In the spring of 1943, one of Florida State's first citizens began his long association with the institution. Dr. Milton Washington Carothers was appointed professor of education and acting registrar. In 1960 he served for five months as acting president of Florida State University following the death of Dr. Robert M. Strozier.

Dr. Carothers's son, the Reverend Milton Stover Carothers, attended FSU (class of 1954) and in 1982 donated his collection of rare books to Strozier Library in honor of his father and his mother, Julia Stover Carothers. At the presentation of the collection, Daisy Parker Flory slyly but sincerely honored the character of this couple who did so much for FSU:

I can say that I have never heard a critical or disparaging comment about Milton or Julia. This is a unique observation I can make about no others prominent in this university, which I have known fairly well since 1933. It is truly remarkable, almost incredible. The university community is trained for questioning, analyzing, dissecting—critiquing—and it likes to exercise to keep fit.

As early as 1929, there was talk of making Florida State College for Women coeducational. Around campus, it was one of those titillating topics that editors of the student-run *Florida Flambeau* liked to raise occasionally just for kicks. Few before 1941 actually took the idea seriously. But dramatic world events that year forced change.

Less than three miles west of Landis Green, the Army Air Corps had set up a base for pilot training. By the fall of 1942, more than 2,000 male trainees were living at Dale Mabry Field, a tantalizing development to be sure.

The impact on FSCW was both predictable and swift. Both President Doak Campbell and Olivia Dorman, dean of students, realized that a ban on all contact between the student body and the new male neighbors would be futile. To keep a grip on the new social dynamic, Campbell and Dorman set up a regular series of formal dances in the Longmire Building. Throngs of men in uniform became familiar Saturday-night sights at these and other "soldier parties" thrown by the administration.

For the next few years, life at FSCW was suffused with such manifestations of war. Most male teachers of draft age vanished. Enrollment shot upward, as young women sought training to help their families cope with missing wage-earners. The student body rallied to do its bit for the war effort, including planting victory gardens, knitting clothes, rolling bandages and selling war bonds.

All in all, it was a time of great excitement. Aside from their new social dimension (something their parents hadn't counted on), the women were awakened to the more sobering realities of wartime. The near-coastal Tallahassee was regarded as being subject to German bombing attacks. Air raid sirens were installed on the roofs of Landis Hall and Westcott, and students soon learned to scramble for shelter when they heard them wail. The shooting war became real in June of 1942, when a German U-boat torpedoed and sank the 430 foot British tanker *Empire Mica* off Apalachicola.

As the Allied war machine approached final victory, the G.I. Bill threatened to swamp campuses nationwide with returning vets. At the all-male university in Gainesville, the situation was intolerable by summer of 1946. UF President J. J. Tigert announced that 8,400 men had applied for the fall term—2,200 more than there was room for.

A special joint meeting of the Boards of Control and Education was held in Tallahassee on Sept. 2, 1946 (Labor Day) to discuss the situation. President Campbell was pressed to consider the urgency of the situation and grant access to FSCW classes to as many men as practical. They could be housed in the old Dale Mabry barracks, recently acquired by the city, which was willing to donate the property to the campus. If the cabinet and boards could immediately cut loose funds for hiring more faculty and renovating housing, Campbell saw no problem.

The very next morning, the cabinet met and approved a plan to install up to 1,000 male students at FSCW during the coming year. To make this two-day deal legal—state law specifically prohibited coeducation at FSCW—the Board of Control created "TBUF," the Tallahassee Branch of the University of Florida. State Attorney General Tom Watson quibbled, saying that the emergency measure should in no way be construed as "a precedent" for coeducation at FSCW. Campbell replied that whatever the technicalities may be, in reality FSCW was now Florida's first *de facto* coed institution of higher learning.

By the spring of 1947, Tallahassee-born Senator Leroy Collins was ready with a bill effectively overhauling the state's antiquated higher-ed system. Howls of protest by loyal University of Florida partisans punctuated lively debate on the issue, but on May 7, 1947, Collins's bill passed both houses. With the stroke of a pen, on May 15 Governor Caldwell transformed Florida State College for Women—with its four generations of rich, liberal-arts tradition—into Florida State University.

Excerpted from "The Great Transition" by Frank Stephenson, *Research in Review.* Information for the article was drawn from *Femina Perfecta: The Genesis of Florida State University* by Robin Jeanne Sellers, Ph.D. This dissertation, representing the first comprehensive history of FSCW and its transition to FSU, was published in 1995 as a book by the FSCW/FSU Class of 1947.

Caroline Pruitt Ransom
(class of 1947)

It was time to register for courses for the second semester in the winter of 1945. I was standing in the registration line when someone came and told me that my high school sweetheart, Bill Ransom, was missing in action in Europe.

Six months later Bill was found in a German prison camp by the conquering Allied Army.

Bill used to come to FSCW and later FSU to see me, spending the nights in the old Dale Mabry barracks.

We married in 1949 and have three children. Our youngest son, Nathaniel, graduated from FSU, as did his wife, the former Selena Fleskes.

Above: Caroline Pruitt in her FSCW dorm room
Below: Caroline's brother Tom Pruitt was commissioned at nineteen, served in the army throughout the war, and left the service when he was twenty-three. He often visited his sisters Caroline (R) and Mary Lynn at FSCW.

The Pseudopodalists, a social group, pose in front of Westcott c.1953. George Milton (in beret) and Dorothy Dean earned money painting clown shoes for the FSU circus. The group also included Andre Jullian, Evon Streetman, Russ West, Cynthia Sweat, Bunn Gray, Erin Sessions, Eb Thomas, Jeannie Hotard, Franklin Adams, James van Emerson, Janey Rhyne Middlebrooks, Dorothy Womble and Dorothy Kannon.

Daisy Parker Flory (1942–1984)

Professor of Political Science and Dean of the Faculties Emerita

Daisy Parker Flory, whose career began at FSCW in 1942, retired from FSU in 1984 with these words: "The whole business has been fun; these forty-two years have been happy ones." During that time she taught Florida government to students who went on to govern the state, was dean of faculties since the creation of the position, and served twice as acting vice-president for academic affairs.

Daisy Flory's affiliation with the university really encompassed sixty-five years. As an undergraduate at FSCW from 1933 to 1937, she was an honor student in history, a member of Phi Beta Kappa and Mortar Board, and a student senator. She also worked on the staff of the *Flambeau*, edited the literary magazine, and was chairman of the handbook committee. She always believed that the strong liberal arts tradition of FSCW made FSU the liberal arts institution in the state, a heritage to cherish.

Physics professor Steve Edwards, who succeeded Daisy Flory as dean of faculties, said that her contributions to the university were endless: "To me, one of the most important of these was her leadership in maintaining the strong role played by faculty in the governance of the university. This set the character of the institution and is the greatest source of its strength."

Even after retirement Daisy and her husband, retired English professor Claude Flory, continued their relationship with FSU. Always a strong supporter of women's athletics, she continued to attend games, supporting them both administratively and personally. "I've always been busy," she said with a smile, "and I expect to remain so."

Florida State, February 1985

Jesse Earle Bowden (class of 1951): On Returning to Tallahassee in 2001

Suddenly, I'm eighteen again, living in a former Army Air Corps barracks at Dale Mabry Field—a human fragment from the post-World War II beginnings of Florida State University. Fresh out of Altha High School I was in a man-swarm of war veterans in Army khaki, Navy dungarees, and paratroop boots, talking about the Big War as beer flowed on West Campus.

Across Tallahassee's hills, reachable by a fleet of buses, was an intellectual bastion of womanhood, an ivy-laced academy with a long, socially regimented tradition as Florida State College for Women. Not that the male species was unknown. During World War II, Army Air Corps pilots—including Chinese airmen—were trained at nearby Dale Mabry Field. And more than 400 FSCW graduates served in the war, including Lt. Marion Phillips, class of 1932, killed when a plane in which she was a passenger crashed into an Italian mountainside.

By war's end, Dale Mabry Field was closed, the hotshot pilots leaving, and a *Florida Flambeau* headline lamented: "Dateless Saturdays Threaten When Flyers Leave Town." FSCW had grown so fast since 1943 that even women had temporary housing in four Dale Mabry buildings. Meanwhile, in Gainesville, an astounding number of men wanted to enroll in the University of Florida, 2,800 more than the school could handle.

President Doak Campbell agreed to teach a thousand men if the state furnished living quarters and money for additional faculty. Thus was born the Tallahassee Branch of the University of Florida (TBUF), with Dr. Milton Carothers, FSCW registrar, made dean.

Some 600 men were enrolled. And the infamous former Air Force Major Otis McBride became dean of men. A summons from McBride, which was frequent, became known as a "Notice from Otis."

It was a strange new world. Suddenly ex-G.I.s, single and married, occupied wooden barracks and hung out at the old officers' club, the student O Club. Here a Pensacolian known as Rube Askew emerged as a popular campus politician.

But FSU, or "Tally U" as some would label it, was on the near horizon. Students squeezed into Governor Caldwell's office in the old capitol, applauding the signing of the bill establishing Florida State University on May 15, 1947.

We argued about athletic names from a long, widely circulated list sponsored by the *Flambeau*—Crackers, Rebels, Statesmen, Tarpons, Fighting Warriors, Seminoles. Some of the names didn't make the final cut—Polly-Wogs, Sunshiners, Red Tide, Galloping Gophers, Swamprats, Tallywhackers. But, fortunately, we chose Seminoles, winning by 110 votes.

And naturally there would be football, a dream from the beginning. The yearling athletic department was under Dr. Howard Danforth, who assembled the staff, including Don Veller in 1948, later a talented golf coach and writer. The first team, under coach Ed Williamson, battled Stetson University in Centennial Field in October 1947.

I remember first walking into the Longmire Building and asking Editor Helen Hobbs if I could join the *Flambeau* staff.

I remember sitting in Westcott auditorium listening to folk singer Burl Ives. I remember sitting on the Music Building steps with my future wife, Louise. And I remember the great Flying High Circus, a symphony of athletic skill and beauty.

Today, in another century, I remember returning in the 1970s for the enrollment of our son Steve and going back to the Sweet Shop and a familiar face behind the food counter smiling and saying, "Yes, Earle and Louise, two veal cutlets."

And even now, I still hear Doug Bonifay's ageless chant: FSU one time! FSU two times! FSU three times!

All Female Dance Band, c.1945

"Each month, a social gathering was held in the two sunken gardens in front of Bryan Hall. Selected faculty were invited to attend these evening events. I wore a tuxedo, and the women students came dressed in formal gowns."

ELSTON E. (STEVE) ROADY (1947–1983), PROFESSOR EMERITUS, DEPARTMENT OF POLITICAL SCIENCE

Russell Reaver (1947–1985),

Professor Emeritus, Department of English

These excerpts are taken from the Department of History's oral history project. Nancy Duke interviewed Dr. Reaver in 1989.

I began teaching in the English Department in the fall of 1947, with the first class at the Florida State University. It was the first time that classes could be called "university" classes in Tallahassee.

When I was preparing to become a college professor the beginning salary for an instructor in English was about $1,000 a year. Some of the older and more established professors on campus made $6,000. That was a top salary. . . .

My office was in the "History Building." History was a leading department within the College of Arts and Sciences. It was mainly on one side of the so-called Williams Building, which was next to what is now the Diffenbaugh Building. When Diffenbaugh was constructed I was told that the planners intended it for the foreign language departments so that there could be a rapport between the professors of foreign languages and English. They planned to have a passageway from Diffenbaugh to Williams, but the covered walkway just dead ends. The planners hadn't realized that they would run into a lavatory in Williams where they planned to put the door. So they left the bathroom and never connected the hallway.

When I first came to FSU I was put in a "bullpen" with twenty or twenty-five professors of English. Even if you were a full professor you didn't have a private office; you had a desk. If you had to meet privately with a student, you could go into a classroom or go over to the Sweet Shop. . . .

I was the first professor of English at FSU to be a major professor for a doctoral student. . . . Frances Ethridge Oakes wrote a study of the French reception of Walt Whitman.

"I've determined to view institutions as great theatre with marvelous characters—if you can get beneath their facades," our old friend Harrison Chase said one evening.

He was chatting from his bed at Tallahassee Memorial's extended care center, where he was regaining strength from treatment for lung cancer. He had very much liked the nurses and aides who made the last hours of his own life story more engaging. He observed their activities as he had so many scenes in his life, with a benevolent kind of curiosity. Harrison taught geography at Florida State University for decades—was the first faculty member hired in 1947 just after it had given up its identity as Florida State College for Women. It was natural that he, as with so many in this university town, would take a scholar's look at life.

"She's quiet tonight," he confided as an attendant left the room with her professional mask in place. "She's really very kind and has had a hard struggle." It was if he were orating *Our Town*, speaking of a player walking briefly on the stage and off again.

Certainly in his eighty-six years, Harrison had seen a lot of hidden drama, and some overt. The bewildering stupidity of man, unintended consequences playing out from misguided decisions, a lot of human willingness to hurt one another. . . .

Harrison never failed to see pure comedy, either. He never told jokes but he was intensely witty and wry and . . . more often amused than dismayed by the news of the day.

As a geographer, Harrison understood continents far and wide, but he studied the road maps of human faces well, and when his friends gathered at his memorial service we all felt that we had been special to him. . . . We all liked his keen ability to notice our bright and sparkling sides and view our dark terrain as merely fascinating.

"In his manners and breadth of knowledge and his patience with people, I always wanted to be more like him," said Paul Piccard, a political scientist and Harrison's Saturday morning chess partner. "He had a great ability to see things from other people's perspectives, and he held a very deep, optimistic view of things."

Journalists are always thrilled by the succinct so I cherished one of Harrison's tenets: "There are two kinds of people: those who like to say yes, and those who like to say no." He was one who said yes, but he also asked a lot of whys.

He was the most widely read person most of us had ever known, and his son, Vernon Chase, said wryly that out of deference to his father, he had spent his whole life "trying to hide my superior intellect." We all laughed. We had felt that same awe that his son had from boyhood when he and his buddies would track down old dad to ask a question, "and then go with him on a journey to the answer."

Once Harrison said that if by some happenstance the world would be so damaged that every public library were lost, mankind would not suffer too badly if his own books survived.

He was himself a constructive editor, an extraordinary letter writer and a publisher who, with brother Bill Chase in Ann Arbor, Michigan, published for many years a popular library reference tool called *Chase's Annual Events*.

Tallahassee is known above all for its professors, students, and countless lifetimes devoted to education. It is the perfect venue to salute one who reached the pinnacle of his profession—yet never earned a doctorate.

Mary Ann Lindley, *Tallahassee Democrat*, February 20, 2000

Edna Campbell, wife of the president, shows students bees she cultivated.

Dean of Women
Katherine Warren
(class of 1933) serving
punch at President
Doak Campell's house.

Change was the most constant campus theme of spring 1947. To begin with, 600 men enrolled at Tallahassee Branch, University of Florida (TBUF), housed at Dale Mabry Field, an act that *Flastacowo* felt put the college "well on the way to reconversion toward coeducation."

All spring long a debate over coeducation raged across the campus. The *Flambeau* militantly backed the idea. Its masthead proclaimed: "Early Legislation for Coeducation."

The two honoraries, Esteren (Evens) and Spirogira (Odds), held a student poll on the subject and found that FSCW women voted 1,803 to 114 in favor of the change. TBUF men were slightly more in favor. They voted "aye" by 350–0. To buttress its position, the *Flambeau* printed faculty opinion. Daisy Parker said, "It seems to me that coeducation is not only desirable, but inevitable."

As the battle raged there was much business as usual. Cultural opportunities were never better. Jan Peerce gave a concert in May, Eve Curie lectured on "The Magic of Radium," and an exhibition of thirty-five Diego Rivera drawings was held in Longmire.

Despite this activity, coeducation was the topic on all lips. On May 7 campus proponents were jubilant as the Florida House passed Representative Bourke Floyd's coed bill 80–7 and the Senate assented unanimously. Eight days later at 9:50 a.m. Governor Millard Caldwell signed the bill and an era ended. Both FSCW and the University of Florida were coeducational. Equally important, FSCW now had full status as a university. Later that year, with a mixture of nostalgia and hope, members of the Florida State community watched as workmen took down "Florida State College for Women" and replaced it with "Florida State University" in the archway between the Westcott gates.

When a spanking new Florida State University opened for business in the fall of 1947, 4,400 students signed up — double the enrollment of fall 1945. Of the enrollees, 1,054 were men, and 890 of these were paying their way on the G.I. Bill. Interestingly, 25 G.I. Bill students enrolling that first semester in '47 were women.

Dick Puckett (L) and Ed Franklin (in FSU shirts) in the Sweet Shop

Student Union, 1949

Alice Cromartie Cassels (class of 1948)

1944–45: Arriving on a very large campus from a small farming community was very exciting. It was comforting to have a structured routine, even though breaking rules caused me to have to appear, once or twice, before the House Council.

The effects of World War II were felt. Bacon was served once a week or less, and we could smell it in the freshman dorms. Suddenly someone would run down the hall shouting "B-Day!" which meant bacon on the cafeteria line. Then came the great exodus, raincoats over rolled-up pajamas to claim the treat. I wonder if Miss Tracy ever knew how popular she was those mornings and how we had dressed for the occasion.

Sunday night picnic suppers were popular too. All of the ice cold milk you could carry in whatever container you had and as many FSCW icebox cookies as your hands could hold went with you back to the dorm. Sandwiches were also available but were not as popular.

1945–46: Returning to campus following the summer break was fun. There were new rumors about men being admitted to FSCW.

1946–47: It was hard to believe we were juniors, the time had flown so quickly. Free of basic studies we moved purposefully into our major fields of study. Grade point averages went up, and gone for good were two years of Latin and Dr. Harold Richards, who successfully combined terror and physics. The downside was leaving humanities classes and Dr. Hudson Rogers. The big news on campus in the spring of 1947 was that the Legislature was changing FSCW to FSU and that lots of guys would be studying in our hallowed halls. Anticipation was off the Richter scale!

Suddenly we arrived at graduation day and the future we knew was out there somewhere. I recall writing my dean a letter from Boston, where I was interning, letting her know that FSU had fully prepared me for everything I needed to handle. That's the real reason to be forever grateful to FSU.

Elston E. (Steve) Roady (1947–1983), Professor Emeritus, Department of Political Science

In June of 1947 I was at the University of Illinois and looking for a teaching job. The placement office had a listing for a job at Florida State University, and I applied. The opportunity to get in on the ground floor of a new political science department at a newly coed school was tempting. I had been in the area of Tallahassee during WW II and knew it was a beautiful place. A week after sending my credentials to Dr. Marian D. Irish, chair of the Department of Political Science, I received a telegram offering me a position as an instructor that would pay $3,500 for a twelve-month appointment. I was married with a baby daughter, Beth, so I sent a return telegraph saying I would accept if assured of housing. The next day I got a reply, signed Doak S. Campbell, President, assuring me housing.

After arriving by train at the Thomasville, Georgia, railroad station on September 5, 1947, at 5:30 a.m., we took a cab to the Cherokee Hotel in Tallahassee. Later that morning I went to campus, and the next day we were taken to our "housing" on the West Campus, formerly the Dale Mabry Army Air Corps Base. Within a day we were established in a two-story barracks located at the end of Roberts Avenue, our part being the upstairs west-side. Our furnishings were minimal, and my wife Barbara did the washing in the tub. The subsidized housing, which included everything except for the telephone, cost us $35 each month.

Each month, a social gathering was held in the two sunken gardens in front of Bryan Hall. Selected faculty were invited to attend these evening events. I wore a tuxedo, and the women students came dressed in formal gowns. In each sunken garden a centerpiece table held a beautiful silver or cut glass bowl filled with a delicious drink. Surrounding the bowls were flowers, finger foods, crackers, cheeses, and fruit. It was a very pleasant way to mingle with students.

FSU hired 111 faculty members in that class of 1947 which, like the class of 1949, provided outstanding scholars that helped to give FSU its high standing in the academic world.

The 1949 Florida legislative session reflected the grave concerns and fears of communism common in the country, which was uneasy with its relations with the USSR. Special committees in both the Florida House and Senate were established to "protect" the students from suspect professors. Night hearings were held, and at one both Charles Clapp and I were held accountable. When some of our students protested, they were promptly removed from the room. The outcome of these hearings was the passage of a loyalty oath and further field investigations of faculty members. We became suspect in terms of our perceived leanings toward communism, atheism, and homosexuality. I was determined not to sign the loyalty oath but was finally persuaded by my wife because otherwise I would have lost my position at FSU. The legislature sent each of us a sixteen-page document that we had to sign and arranged for us to have fingerprints and mug shots made. Never mind that I had received a top-secret clearance from the U.S. military, with my picture and fingerprints already on file.

When I took early retirement in 1984 I realized that, although I received more than adequate recognition for my academic work in political science, my greatest love had been to teach the young women and men who came my way.

When Doak Campbell set to work transforming what he called "a splendid undergraduate college" into "a university in fact," with first-class graduate education, his first step was department- and faculty-building, particularly in the sciences. Heading a nationwide search for talent, University of Chicago–trained Edwin R. Walker arrived on campus at the start of the 1948–49 academic year as dean of the College of Arts and Sciences. Additions were made to the teaching staff in 1947 and 1948 as well as in the 1950s, but they reached a peak in 1949 with approximately 125 additions. These latter newcomers became known as 49ers.

So complete was the transformation from FSCW by 1957 that Robert M. Strozier, succeeding Campbell as president, called what had been done "one of the miracles of the academic world." The 49ers provided much of the heft needed in this transformation.

Clifton Paisley, *Research in Review*, February 1979

"I gave [Walker] as near carte blanche *as I have ever given anybody in the location and attraction of young men who were highly trained in the branches of science to which we expected to give attention."*

PRESIDENT DOAK CAMPBELL

Before Edwin R. Walker came to FSU as dean of the College of Arts and Sciences, he was a professor of philosophy at the University of Colorado. Forget stereotypes of metaphysical meanderings. By the time Walker arrived on campus for the start of the '48 fall semester, he already had a well-planned agenda, which could have been summed up in a single phrase: bring on the science.

Sensing the school's potential for rapid growth—thousands of education-starved ex-G.I.s were finding precious little science training in the South—Walker became a national headhunter for young talent in the sciences. He chose to go after promising Ph.D. graduates just starting their teaching careers, figuring he couldn't compete against well-established universities seeking seasoned faculty members.

In 1971, shortly before he died, Campbell said: "I gave [Walker] as near *carte blanche* as I have ever given anybody in the location and attraction of young men who were highly trained in the branches of science to which we expected to give attention."

Walker's passion for hiring bright young scientists was matched by his determination to set a new tone for scholarship on campus. Kitty Hoffman, who taught chemistry at FSCW and at the new university before retiring in 1984, remembers the Walker years and the effect his leadership had on faculty: "It was made clear to the faculty that they had to take certain steps toward getting their Ph.D., or they would not be advanced," she recalls. "Teaching, then, would no longer be all that was required."

When Ed Walker took up the reins for leading Florida State into the ranks of consequential universities in 1948, he couldn't have picked a better time for such a job anywhere on the continent.

Before the war, a college sheepskin was a rare animal—less than two percent of the population owned one. Two-thirds of the men and women who served in the war had not even completed high school.

And suddenly, here comes Uncle Sam offering 16 million eligible vets a free ticket for something their mommas and daddies had only dreamed of—a college degree. So, just when Walker went shopping for young academics with advanced training, the G.I. Bill was producing them wholesale.

Walker wasn't on the job three months before the young university had its first cohesive policy governing research activities and a research council. By 1950, Walker had hired more than 200 faculty (with brilliant choices in the arts and humanities too). In April the university joined its first research consortium, the Oak Ridge Institute of Nuclear Studies.

In 1950, Florida's Board of Control granted FSU its first doctoral programs in science—in chemistry, physiology/zoology, and botany. A Ph.D. in meteorology was available in 1952, as was a terminal degree in psychology. A doctorate in physics followed in 1953.

News began to spread about the rigorous science-course offerings at the former "girl's school" in Tallahassee, and enrollment steadily eased upward. The university's tenth anniversary in 1957 was celebrated by 6,700 students—a 200 percent increase in a decade.

Growth meant more infrastructure money from the Legislature—much welcomed by the FSU community as a whole and cheered loudly by the science faculty, who felt they were still living out of boxes. Werner Herz remembers that the chemistry faculty were squeezed onto a single floor in the Science Building (now Diffenbaugh), built in 1921. His "so-called research laboratory" was located five miles away on the West Campus, actually wood-frame barracks.

"The barracks was heated by a coal furnace located in a little hut on the outside," Herz recalled. "In the winter, I had to stoke the furnace myself. In the summer, it was so hot that my solvents [lab chemicals] would evaporate."

Equipment was another story altogether. Without mountains of wartime leftovers to draw from, some labs might never have been built. For years, a war-surplus wind vane, mounted atop a Westcott tower, announced to the world that FSU had a meteorology program.

But after a decade of hard work, state appropriations for FSU had vaulted from $4.8 million in 1947 to $15.4 million 10 years later. In 1955, a Democrat from Tallahassee, staunch FSU-advocate Leroy Collins, was elected to the state house, and FSU's star was on the rise politically as well as academically.

Collins is generally credited with steering a $5 million package

through the 1957 Legislature that established an FSU program in nuclear research. Anchored by a $2 million tandem Van de Graaff nuclear accelerator—at the time one of only two on an American campus—this program instantly became a magnet for highly trained faculty and handsome research dollars. Within ten years of its operation, the nuclear program had generated in federal grants nearly five times its original cost to Florida taxpayers.

Florida State University's name had finally become linked with serious science, and a special kind of science at that. The university became recognized as a center for basic—as opposed to applied— research, work directed more at finding out how natural processes work than in finding immediately useful things to do with them.

Ed Walker's Florida State legacy is prominently evinced by the nationally and internationally acclaimed science programs now seated on campus. Even FSU's $100 million National High Magnetic Field Laboratory, with its far-flung research initiatives in materials science and biotechnology, may rightly be viewed as an outgrowth of strong programs in chemistry and physics which Walker helped start.

Frank Stephenson, excerpted from "War Child," *Research in Review*, Summer 1995

Edwin Walker, an influential dean of Arts and Sciences from 1949 to 1952

Gregg Phifer (1949–1989),

Professor Emeritus, Department of Communications

I completed my doctorate at the University of Iowa in July 1949. Since Clarence Edney at FSU wanted me to begin a debate program, I chose it over another school and reported here September 1 with 125 other 49ers. We made the transition between a fine liberal arts college, inherited from FSCW, and a research university. Most newcomers specialized in one of several natural sciences, but those of us in the humanities and social sciences tagged along. A self-respecting university had to have us too.

For a year or two we had more classroom space on our West Campus, a former military base, than on our present campus. In the summer of '49 the large English Department set up headquarters on West Campus and Wayne Minnick and I moved into one of the offices they left in 201 Williams.

The University of Florida was delighted to become coeducational but thought we should remain a college for women. The Legislature disagreed, but at least UF could try preventing us from developing a football program. Florida's old Board of Control was divided on that subject, but the chair's vote made it 3–2 to leave that decision to President Campbell. And he said that a self-respecting university had to have a football team.

Football was not our only intercollegiate sport in that first FSU year. I remember attending and taking some slides of a dual track meet between FSU and the University of Miami on our old West Campus track. By the next year I had volunteered to officiate, a habit I have maintained to the present 2001.

A year or two later it was suggested that I have a debate assistant. An application for graduate study came from Betty Flory, then the debate and drama coach at Edgewater High School in Orlando. She had excellent credentials. So FSU gave Betty an assistantship to help with debate, and for two years I was her boss. Then in 1956 we got married and switched roles.

Vaughn Mancha played football for the University of Alabama (1945–1948). A member of the FSU Sports Hall of Fame, he was a coach and athletic director at FSU.

King and queen of the junior-senior prom court, Reubin Askew and Faye Patterson, 1951

Cheerleaders, 1947 to 1948

We—my husband Earl, two small children, and I—arrived in Tallahassee on Labor Day, 1949, after an exhausting six-day drive from Los Angeles in a 1939 Chevrolet. The housing that had been found for us was a unit at the old El Rancho Motel on West Tennessee Street. It was about six o'clock in the evening, hot and humid. There was no air conditioning so we decided to go to sleep and tackle our new life in the morning.

Our first mission was to explore the town. We drove down Monroe Street looking for downtown Tallahassee and instead found a city limits sign just beyond the capitol. Then we went looking for the public library. We found a large white building that looked promising but that turned out to be a private residence.

Our five-year old daughter started school the next day, Earl went to the university, and I was left to make order out of the unbelievable chaos of boxes, bags and dirty clothes left from the trip. Fortunately one of the few necessities that we brought with us was the potty-chair upon which my son Jimmy was sitting when the door-bell rang. There stood three beautiful ladies in flowered dresses and white gloves come to welcome us to Tallahassee, to FSU, and more specifically to the Department of Chemistry. At that moment Jimmy yelled that he was "all through," which I thought described my life perfectly. Kitty Hoffman, the lead lady, and I still share vivid memories of that moment.

As Earl was no longer an impoverished grad student, but was now an impoverished faculty member, we thought we should be able to serve drinks to guests when we entertained. To that end I went to Bennett's drug store to ask about purchasing some bourbon. The salesgirl said, "Honey, this is a drah caounty." I had trouble understanding anything she said.

I thought the eighteenth amendment had been repealed and knew nothing at that time about county options. I finally understood when she directed me to a bootlegger just beyond the city limits sign. I was shocked that she would think I would do something illegal. The city limits sign was beginning to play a large part in my life.

At FSU Earl was having his own problems. His research was on metamorphosis. Tadpoles and frogs were his experimental animals, and he had no tanks in which to house them. His brilliant solution was to scour the town for old houses that were being demolished and to salvage the discarded bath tubs. His lab was soon lined with the claw-footed tubs, painted pink, and the tadpoles had a home. Unfortunately they were dying before they could be used. The problem was the weather; the summer heat was lethal to them. Consequently Earl had the first air-conditioned laboratory in the chemistry department, probably in the entire university.

After three weeks at the motel we found a house to rent on Arkansas Street. The landlord lived next door. He had been using the yard of our house as a vegetable garden and generously offered me the fresh produce. He pointed out the kale, okra and greens. I had never heard of any of it. To me vegetables started with English peas and ended with string beans. I thanked him and told him that he was welcome to the fruits of his labor as I probably wouldn't have time to take proper care of it. This man seemed to live on his front porch. Every time I stepped outside he greeted me with a hearty "Hay," a form of greeting that was new to me and always startling.

Shopping for food was another learning experience. We found a market in the center of town called the Piggly Wiggly, which we called Giggly. They had never heard of sour cream, lox, or bagels, to mention only a few of the staples of our L.A. diet. No California oranges, no artichokes or avocados. It was obviously going to be a whole new way of life.

Department of
Chemistry, faculty and
students, c. 1951

LIFE

'I FOUGHT IN FOREIGN LEGION,'
ADRIAN LIDDELL HART ON INDO-CHINA

A POLISH GIRL D.P. ...

...BECOMES QUEEN
OF A U.S. COLLEGE

20 CENTS

DECEMBER 15, 1952

In 1952 eighteen-year-old Marlies Gessler, a native of Poland, was FSU's homecoming queen and a *Life Magazine* cover girl.

In the spring of 1949, Florida State University was still completing the transition from women's college to major coed university. Men's and women's hospital facilities were combined, and a gala ceremony welcomed Florida State's first fraternities: Pi Kappa Alpha, Alpha Tau Omega, Delta Tau Delta, Phi Kappa Tau, Sigma Alpha Epsilon, Kappa Alpha, and Theta Chi.

To help accommodate the increased student population (1,958 men and 3,185 women), a new wing was added to the East Campus Gym. On hand for the dedication was Katherine Montgomery, honored at the twenty-fifth anniversary of the Department of Physical Education. The gym now bears Miss Montgomery's name.

In May, the FSU student body voted on the university's alma mater as the institution acquired another necessary college tradition. "High o'er the Towering Pines" by Johnny Lawrence, a World War II vet and local musician, won the contest.

The most ominous event of 1949 was McCarthyism, with Florida State University also swept into the midst of a raging national hysteria. On April 29, the *Flambeau* was headlined "House Committee to Investigate Red Activity at FSU. Campbell Welcomes Lawmakers to Probe FSU for Communism." Two weeks later the university community read, "Communist Probe Growing." In a statement typical of the era's sensationalism a report boasted, "House members have indicated that they now have factual information concerning 'red' activities here." The editorial staff of the *Flambeau* struck a rational note in the hysteria with a plea: "Now that the Florida State University communistic investigation has assumed full scale proportions it is to be hoped that necessary precautions will be taken to safeguard the reputations of innocent persons involved."

Many aspects of campus life that spring were business as usual in an American university of the '40s. The Florida State Alumni Association picked a new president—Alma Warren, the wife of Florida Governor Fuller Warren—and radio station WFSU began its career of bringing music to the Tallahassee community. On May 7 the first track meet ever held at Florida State saw Ken Miller's thinclads lose to Mississippi College 70–60.

One issue that produced a divided campus was the compulsory wearing of rat caps. The university council took up the issue and voted against the compulsion by a narrow 6–5 count. With the majority was student body president Ed Eissey. One of the minority five was a council member from Pensacola named Rube Askew.

On June 6, 1949, 453 graduates walked into Westcott to receive their degrees. This class marked what the *Flambeau* called "The End of an Era." The article noted that: "The 1949 graduating class is the last class that entered into a completely women's FSCW. So with hearts grateful for the past experiences of our older sister college, we say goodbye to the last remnants of that era and turn with anticipation to see what the future holds for Florida State University."

"Hungarian Ernst von Dohnányi was until 1960, the year of his death, a professor of music at Florida State University and was enchanted with so unlikely a base of cultural operations as Tallahassee, where his students were apt to greet him with 'Hey, Maestro, you got on sharp socks today!' 'Learn to play in the dark,' he admonished them. 'Florida has frequent power failures.'"

GLORIA JAHODA, *RIVER OF THE GOLDEN IBIS*, UNIVERSITY PRESS OF FLORIDA, 1973

Richard M. Baker (1950–1981), Professor Emeritus, Marketing

I drove into Tallahassee on the last day of February, 1950, and began my first day at FSU on the first day of March. I was employed by Dr. Hazel Stevens, chair, Department of Clothing and Textiles, to develop a retail training program for students aspiring to careers in merchandising. I worked with retailers throughout the state in instituting an intern program in which students worked in stores under my academic supervision. I also developed and taught courses. By 1955 the program was maturing, students were finding management level jobs in the industry, and enrollments were increasing, so I accepted the position of director, FSU Bootstrap Program at Eglin AFB, Florida. In 1957 I returned to teaching in the School of Business, later the College of Business.

I served as assistant dean for graduate studies under dean of business Ray Solomon, and also taught marketing. In 1976 I was asked to serve as chairman of the Marketing Department and in 1979 became associate dean for development, a position I held until I retired in June of 1981.

The most fun I had in my later years on campus was serving as chairman of the Athletic Board. I joined the board in 1970 and within a few months was named chairman upon the retirement of Dean Stone of the College of Education. The athletic program was on shaky ground in the early seventies. Football coach Bill Peterson resigned, and we brought in Larry Jones. When the next coach, Darrell Mudra, had several dismal seasons, we gave serious thought to giving up the football program. In late 1975 I headed a small search committee to find a coach who could save the program. We selected Bobby Bowden. As the saying goes, the rest is history.

I have watched the university grow from a small, comfortable, quiet campus to the giant institution it is today. Although I came to campus six months later than the so-called 49ers, I count myself one of them. We are credited with launching the university on its journey to where it is today. I am proud of my small contribution.

In the fall of 1998, the Marching Chiefs honored Tommy Wright for his fifty years of teaching at FSU. In 1950 Wright wrote "FSU Fight Song" to words by Doug Alley. Alley is retired as a professor of English at Auburn University.

James B. Tippen, Jr. (class of 1950)

This is an excerpt from James B. Tippen's A True Obligation, *a salute to the group of veterans of WW II who gathered at Dale Mabry Field, west of Tallahassee, Florida, in September,1946, to found Tallahassee Branch—University of Florida (TBUF).*

This small band, light in spirit and expectation, with little to recommend them to the academy, were to become a vital part of the nucleus from which, in a matter of months, came The Florida State University.

Building 641 was a typical, generic U.S. Army structure, sitting high in the air atop cinder block pylons. . . . A denim-clad fellow of enhanced chronology glowered from the steps. I assumed he was a carpenter, for, after all, he was holding a folding ruler and a carpenter's flat pencil. A regular old #2 was held in reserve by the band of his perspiration-dyed Devoe paint cap. To his growling "Where do you want to live kid?," I replied, "Building number 641." His crusty face broke into a half-smile, that knowing hard-to-come-by smile. With hands in his pockets, and after a spit with a trajectory of which the 8th Infantry would be envious, he moistly said, "No, college boy, inside this building."

Inside I became aware that the four outside walls were the whole of Building 641. Seeing a window, I asked, "Why not here?" His only response was, "Why not?" He unfolded his ruler, drew a rectangle on the floor with the broad point of his carpenter's pencil, and began to nail 2-by-4 studs in conformity with his penciled lines. I stood for a while awaiting the completion of my room. The walls were made of something called "beaver board" made of pressed sugar cane. They were in place within thirty minutes.

Jimmy Joanos, a Tallahassee native, received his degree from Florida State University in Public Administration in 1956. After three years in the Air Force he added a law degree from Yale University.

At FSU in the fifties Joanos was president of the Sigma Chi House, president of Omicron Delta Kappa, a member of Gold Key, and vice-president of the student body. He fondly recalls these years, remembering the smaller, more intimate campus. He knew most of his fellow students and remains grateful to the faculty members who provided his foundation for Yale Law School: Drs. Daisy Parker Flory, Marian Irish, Paul Piccard, Malcolm Parsons, and Vince Thursby.

At Yale Joanos joined FSU friends Pete Nimkoff and Bob Canada in law school. He remembers that the Florida State trio felt well prepared for the challenge. In 1962 Joanos was elected secretary of his class at Yale.

FSU's Gold Key chapter gave Joanos its Outstanding Alumnus Award in 1967, and that same year he was chosen one of the five Outstanding Young Men of Florida. In 1968 Joanos was elected president of the Tallahassee Chamber of Commerce and two years later became national president of the FSU Alumni Association.

In 1971 Joanos became a judge of the Leon County Felony Court of Record, then circuit judge of the Second Judicial Circuit of Florida. On January 1, 2001, he retired as a judge of the Florida First District Court of Appeal.

As his legal career flourished in Tallahassee, Joanos remained actively involved in alumni affairs. When he says, "Florida State is a part of me, I am a part of the Florida State family," he means it literally. His wife, the former Betty Lou Whittle, his two brothers and his sister, his twin daughters and his son are all FSU grads. Betty Lou is also a great supporter of FSU, personally and professionally, as the associate director of Alumni Affairs.

An accomplished amateur photographer and an avid sports fan, Joanos saw Florida State's initial football game in 1947 and has missed very few home games since.

1952: "Madam President" Redux, Olympics at Last

Second semester registration counted 5,100 students on campus. Construction in process included women's and men's dorms (Dorman and Smith) and a student union containing a post office.

The United States was still involved in the Korean "police action," and a major point of discussion in the existing and eight new fraternities was "Will I get drafted?"

That spring Mary Rupth Summers became the first woman elected student body president since the arrival of coeducation.

Famed FSU music professor Ernst von Dohnányi gave a piano recital and joined violinist Albert Spalding in a concert. Metropolitan Opera baritone Leonard Warren sang in May, and the new music building was named Opperman Hall after longtime music dean Ella S. Opperman.

Early 1952 brought mixed athletic news. The basketball team ended one of the university's worst campaigns with a 5–20 record. However, in gymnastics, Hartley Price's team won its second consecutive NCAA championship. FSU's Bill Roetzheim and Don Holder were named to the U.S. Olympic team for the Helsinki games—the first Seminole athletes in any sport to be so honored.

Florida State, 1982

Members of the FSU School of Nursing deliver Christmas trees to patients at the Tallahassee Memorial Hospital in 1957.

The Flying Seminoles, Dick Puckett and Ed Franklin, made their first appearance at an FSU football game on October 3, 1953. (It was also the first FSU home game for a new sports editor of the *Tallahassee Democrat*, the late Bill McGrotha, in whose memory the Campbell Stadium press box is named.) Over the next four years, Puckett and Franklin became one of the most recognizable symbols of the newly coeducational university. "They really were icons for that time," said Nancy Smith Fichter, retired chairperson of FSU's Dance Department. "You know how we all feel about Renegade now. Well, they started that."

Puckett and Franklin met during the ninth grade at Miami's Jackson High. The band director was impressed by their similar talents for dancing, twirling, and tumbling, and decided to pair them as the Flying Twirlers. As such they honed their act in many spotlights, including the Orange Bowl, shows in Texas, Florida, and New York, and several TV shows.

Puckett and Franklin were recruited to FSU like a pair of blue-chip football players. Numerous colleges offered band scholarships, but they were determined to stay together and held out for a school that would take them both, and FSU would.

The Flying Seminoles performed at seven football games a year for four years.

Their opening routine was always a crowd-pleaser. They came out from opposite end zones before the game and pranced to midfield with "deer jumps"—a dance leap. Then they jumped several feet into the air, butted their chests against each other, and fell spread-eagled on the ground. Before the game, they led the band on the field by turning back-flips the length of the field. But their main stage was half time.

Dashing through three and four costume changes in fifteen minutes, Puckett and Franklin performed choreographed routines to the Marching Chiefs' music. For their first performance in 1953, they wore white tuxedos and danced to Rachmaninoff—the same act they did for their final game November 16, 1956. In between, they accompanied the band's salutes to everything from Broadway to Disney from Glenn Miller to Elvis Presley. They danced with majorettes, juggled balls and clubs, hurled flaming batons into the air, and caught them behind their backs.

"Puckett and Franklin had such incredible presence," said Smith Fichter, who made them the first males she used in her legendary Days of Dance programs.

A replacement duo for the Flying Seminoles lasted less than a season with the Marching Chiefs. Members of FSU's then-prominent gymnastics program began appearing at football games as "Sammy Seminole." But following the demise of the FSU gymnastics program, Sammy Seminole died as a mascot in 1968. It was 1978 before FSU got another Seminole show stopper: Chief Osceola and Renegade, an authentically costumed Seminole rider and Appaloosa horse whose planting of a flaming spear precedes every game.

Both Puckett and Franklin went on to get master's degrees from FSU—and lead similar careers. Puckett spent five years as art director at WFSU television and then was hired as the first director of LeMoyne in 1964. He left in 1974 for fifteen years in private business, owning the popular Shaw's Furniture store for many years. In 1979 he was lured back to LeMoyne, where he worked to turn the gallery into a thriving enterprise.

He was married to the late Joyce Chick Puckett, a retired FSU professor.

Gerald Ensley, *Tallahassee Democrat*, November 1, 1997

Opposite: Dick Puckett (L) and Ed Franklin, here with Paula Parsons at the Orange Bowl, 1955

"*There are no individual stars. You can't participate without good grades. Everyone must share in the work. You have to rig your own act and carry your own equipment. Sound like fun? It is. This is what the FSU Circus is all about. Good grades and a lot of hard work.*"

RICHARD BRINSON, DIRECTOR OF THE FSU FLYING HIGH CIRCUS

The FSU Flying High Circus was founded in 1947 by Jack Haskins, a new faculty member.

Flying High

2001 marks the 54th year of annual home shows for FSU's Flying High Circus. Founded in 1947 by Jack Haskins and now directed by Richard Brinson, the circus features Florida State students who fly, swing, skate, balance, juggle, and clown under one of the largest tents in the country.

Over the years the Florida State Circus has won worldwide acclaim. It has played abroad in Florence, Nice, Barcelona, and Athens as well as performing in Canada and the West Indies.

The Flying DeCosmos

In its early days, a highly celebrated feature of FSU's Flying High Circus was its first flying act, dubbed "The Flying DeCosmos" in honor of the group's founder and coordinator, James (Jim) V. DeCosmo (shown at bottom, looking up). DeCosmo, a '49 graduate of TBUF (Tallahassee Branch of the University of Florida), joined the university's physical education department in 1950 where he taught and worked as an assistant to circus director Jack Haskins. The original Flying DeCosmos, seen here in 1951, are (from top): John Mabey, Sandy Sanderson, Ann Callahan, and Shirley Boulware.

Burt Reynolds (1954–1955)

I said, "Miami plays Nebraska, Notre Dame, and big-time schools. Who does Florida State play? Stetson? Furman?"

"Not next year," Howser said. "They're moving up. It's gonna be Alabama, Auburn, Georgia."

Despite having signed to attend Miami, I visited the Florida State campus. Why not? The rush parties the university threw for prospective athletes were great. And with fourteen scholarship offers, I got to be pretty good at being entertained. I expected to see a pretty little campus covered with ivy, but not such a charming little town. Then I met one of the slickest, most charismatic men I have ever met, and did he do a number on me.

Tom Nugent, the new head coach, was on a mission. Florida State was going into big-time football. He was an innovative genius; he gave football the I-formation, the typewriter huddle, the lonesome end. In those days, most schools passed very little. FSU passed more than it ran. He also made FSU the first team to wear white shoes—not so innovative, but, like everything else he came up with, it's still around.

He was just as clever as a recruiter of talent. Behind his desk hung a beautiful, wide-angled photo of the FSU campus. I didn't pay any attention to it when we first started talking about what Miami was giving me. In those days, there was no reason not to answer candidly. Cars, jobs, money. It was all routine stuff. Coach Nugent was still unfazed by Miami's generosity.

"Buddy, will they give you that?," he asked, swiveling around in his chair and pointing at the school picture. "With your athletic ability and charm—well, son, you'll own this entire campus. You'll start for me as a freshman. You won't start as a freshman at Miami, but that's beside the point. Do you know how many girls there are here?"

"No, sir, I don't," I answered.

He said, "Well, this was a girl's school up until 1948, not that this would have any effect on your decision. But there are fourteen girls for every guy."

Burt Reynolds, From *My Life,* Hyperion, 1994

1955 prom king and queen, Harry Massey and Marlies Gessler

An aerial view of Doak Campbell Stadium, dedication day game, October 28, 1950

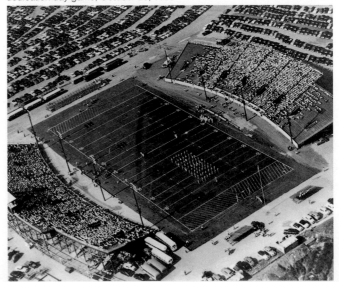

Dr. Grace Fox, a member of the physical education department, was the first woman in America to serve as a member of a university athletic committee governing men's intercollegiate sports. She was appointed to FSU's first six-member committee in 1946 and served for a dozen years in that capacity. She served at a time when FSU first added athletic scholarships, a move some members of the academic community strongly opposed. She remembers the committee as being very aggressive, forward thinking, and wanting to develop a big-time program.

Fox was on the committee when the name Seminoles was adopted. "I remember sitting around the wastepaper basket filled with ballots. We would draw each one out and put it in the appropriate stack," she said. Seminoles was the eventual winner, but not without some early concern that Tarpons might win out. They decided it would be better to have an Indian name than a fish.

"We had an unusual campus just after the war. We had all these cute, pretty freshmen girls and all these old married men [veterans]. So, it wasn't a true campus," Fox laughingly remembered.

Fox said that one of the early concerns after FSCW became FSU was the way the coeds shrank into the background when the men arrived: "We had a very strong girl's school, one of the tops in the nation. There were lots of leadership opportunities. But, when the men came, the ladies didn't want to assume leadership roles any longer. They thought it would make the university seem too 'girl-schoolish.' " The early dilemma was solved by having girls run against girls and men against men in campus elections.

Grace Fox served in the early years by lending her expertise wherever needed. In 1962 she "sewed every stitch" of a giant, gold curtain with eleven panels and the university emblem that hung in Tully gym for many years. The curtain was 30 feet high and contained over 600 yards of material. It was just one of the many remarkable achievements by this exceptional woman.

Vaughn Mancha, *Osceola*, 1996

"We had an unusual campus just after the war. We had all these cute, pretty freshmen girls and all these old married men [veterans]."

GRACE I. FOX

VIRTUOSO implies excellence and versatility in the liberal arts, and at FSC virtuoso implies Mary Lou Norwood. Amazed, we have read her contributions in Distaff and Flambeau; heard her excellent script and subtle puns; admired her poetry, music and paintings, and love for beslacked comfort. An energetic Cotillion president, M'Lu's the genius who produced the superb Junior Minstrels. A conscientious perfectionist, possessed of a bluff generosity (what prop man hasn't depended on the Norwoods as a first or last resort?), Norwood's an idealist to the bone. And beneath her nonchalant and offhand manner is a warm person with a sweetness of her own. Mary Lou puts heart and soul into everything she does and she does everything. She's one of our most dependable and flamboyant personalities. She's the "I Got A Song" girl whose music the whole campus has whistled. She's our girl who's going places.

Left: Mary Lou Norwood (FSCW class of 1947) was interested in anthropology and did volunteer work with the department. She was knowledgeable about local sites of interest.

Right: Albert Martin served as acting president of FSU for a few months after Doak Campbell's retirement in 1957.

"Virtuoso implies excellence and versatility in the liberal arts, and at FSC virtuoso implies Mary Lou Norwood. Amazed, we have read her contributions in Distaff *and* Flambeau, *admired her poetry, music and painting…."*

FLASTACOWO YEARBOOK

James C. Smith (class of 1951), Professor, Department of Psychology:

Memories of Dr. Robert O. Lawton by a Lawton Professor

In the summer of 1951 I completed my M. S. degree in psychology at FSU. The department head, Dr. Hugh Waskom, had an instructor line that he could not fill, so he split it and gave another graduate student and me half-time instructor's positions. During the Korean War in 1953, because I was an "instructor," the university gave me a military leave of absence. This meant that I got a bonus month's pay ($222.22). More important, the university was required to reinstate me (really a graduate student) as an instructor upon my discharge from the Air Force.

That discharge came in May of 1956. Accompanied by my wife, Liz, and our three-month-old son, I took up my duties at Eglin, teaching algebra and general psychology.

Late one afternoon there was a knock on our door. I answered it and the caller said, "Hi, I'm Bob Lawton." We had no idea who he was, and I certainly did not know that he was the director of the Bootstrap Program, hence my boss. We talked about this and that, and because he was familiar with people we knew at the university, Liz and I came to the conclusion that he was somehow associated with FSU.

After a while, Liz asked if he would stay for supper. His response was, "I was beginning to think that you would never ask." When the table was cleared Liz said, "You guys can sit over there and talk if you wish, but I am watching my favorite TV show, *Cheyenne*." That was a sentence Bob Lawton never let Liz forget for the next twenty-five years. We asked Bob if he had a place to spend the night. Again his response was, "I was beginning to think that you would never ask."

A friendship was formed and was deepened over the next three decades. The Lawton kids, Bob Jr. and Lise, were a little older than ours, but they were all close.

[Robert Lawton was killed in an automobile accident in 1980. FSU President Bernard Sliger asked Jim Smith to chair a committee appointed to plan a memorial service for this distinguished and beloved faculty member.]

. . . I remember telling the committee at our first meeting about Elise Lawton's feelings. The solution developed by the committee to meet Bernie's wish for a memorial service and Elise Lawton's wish not to have one was to have a celebration instead. We would name the Distinguished Professorship the Robert O. Lawton Distinguished Professorship, we would appoint the 1981 recipient, Robert Gilmer, in a special service which would be in Bob's memory, and we would celebrate rather than mourn.

In the spring of 1992 President Dale Lick called me and told me that I had been selected as the Robert O. Lawton Professor for the 1992–93 academic year. I was to keep the announcement to myself until commencement. There would have to be one exception. I got in the car and drove to Elise Lawton's. A few weeks later Elise ended her battle with cancer. I will ever be grateful that she knew.

Holding the title of Robert O. Lawton Distinguished Professor still sends shivers down my back. . . . Little did I know in 1956 when I opened the door over in Ft. Walton and heard "Hi, I'm Bob Lawton," what an impact this man would have on my life. Bob's portrait hangs on my outer office wall, and I say goodnight to him every day. I am one blessed person.

Robert O. Lawton was a vice-president for Academic Affairs. The Robert O. Lawton Distinguished Professor award is the highest honor faculty can bestow on a colleague.

PRESIDENTS **ROBERT MANNING STROZIER** (1957–1960),
GORDON W. BLACKWELL (1960–1965),
JOHN E. CHAMPION (1965–1968)

AMAZING GROWTH

President Robert Manning Strozier

President Gordon W. Blackwell

Robert Manning Strozier took over as president of FSU in September 1957 and served until April 1960 when he died suddenly of a heart attack. He had been a popular, respected president whose unexpected death left the university community in shock. Strozier Library was later named in his honor. ¶ Two significant steps forward in science bracketed Dr. Strozier's tenure. In 1957 the Legislature funded a scientifically prestigious Van de Graaff accelerator. This large atom smasher, used for research into atomic nuclei, helped blast FSU's science dreams forward. In 1960 a multimillion-dollar grant from the Atomic Energy Commission established the Institute of Molecular Biophysics. The first of its kind in the Southeast, the institute was chiefly the brainchild of physical chemist Dr. Michael Kasha, who had joined the faculty in 1951 from Berkeley. ¶ On Dr. Strozier's death, Milton Carothers was named acting president. In September 1960, Dr. Gordon Blackwell, formerly the chancellor of the Woman's College of the University of North Carolina, became president of Florida State and served for five years. ¶ In June 1965, John Champion, a member of FSU's business faculty since 1956, stepped forward to join the leadership line. ¶ Any university president of these times—the turbulent sixties—faced unprecedented challenges. Indeed challenge itself became a political and social tenet. To the charge of building a university was to be added defending and defining university life.

President John E. Champion

Opposite: 1958 registration in Tully gym

Tann Hunt (class of 1957)

Tann Hunt practices medical and family law in Tallahassee. In addition to her B.A., she received her Ph.D. (1972) and her J.D. (1982) from Florida State.

Every time I go on campus these days, I am filled with a flood of nostalgia not just for "the good old college days," but for a time of comfort and safety that no longer exists on campus or anywhere else. In the '50s and on into the '60s, it was perfectly safe for a woman of any age to walk unaccompanied on campus and nearby at any time of the day or night (the night controlled by curfew rules!). Seeing the blue emergency phone lights on campus today saddens me greatly.

In 1956 I was a married student with responsibilities going in two directions. As a student, I checked out, one evening, two reserved books from the old library. The rule for such books was that they had to be back in the library by 8:00 a.m. the next morning. Otherwise, they turned into a ticking liability at the rate of 25¢ per hour. Late on that evening, my husband and I received a phone call informing us that my father-in-law was most seriously ill and we should come at once. Without question, or thought for the books, we piled into the car and drove to Pensacola, where we stayed for two or three days.

When we did get back I was faced with returning the books and paying the fine with money which I did not have. I had a reasonable expectation that the library would recognize the emergency and make an exception to the stiff financial penalties. That was not to be. The rather snippy, unpleasant person behind the reserve desk said, "No exceptions." I would have asked once again for an exception, but I was on the verge of tears. Out of seemingly nowhere came a voice, "Take the books back and forget the fine." I turned halfway around and saw nothing. The voice, I discovered, came from a very short woman. I recognized her immediately as someone I had seen before only from a distance but had heard about in tones bordering on veneration. The voice belonged to Dr. Anna Forbes Liddell, professor of philosophy. It was clearly a demonstration that size and might don't make it right; right makes right. I have never forgotten her kindness.

In the early '60s the English Coffee Hour was one of the highlights of my life. Every Friday afternoon, from 4:00 p.m. to 5:00 p.m. in the Presbyterian Students' Center at the corner of Park and Copeland, faculty members (not just in the English Department) spoke or read to those of us caught up in adventures in literature and the humanities. It was intellectually stimulating, socially rewarding, and often a source of fun and laughter as undergraduate and graduate students saw a slightly different side of our faculty and, occasionally, visiting faculty.

In the mid-1950s, female students who ate or drank coffee at the Sweet Shop were often given a flower or a small bouquet by a man about whom we knew nothing. He was short, he was old (to us that was anywhere between fifty and seventy); he always wore gray, usually a sweater even when the weather was warm. He would just extend the flowers, we would say thank you, we would smile at each other, and he walked away. We never had the nerve to ask him who he was or why he did this. Rumor was that he was a retired professor, but we never knew. Except for the flowers, he was a picture of solitude and sadness. It was in a time when he was simply recognized as a kind person rather than, as he might be viewed now, a potential threat.

Martin Dyckman (class of 1957)

Martin Dyckman is associate editor and columnist for the St. Petersburg Times.

I have been a journalist since high school, more than fifty years ago. Only once have I suppressed a story. That was at Florida State University.

However, we must begin at the beginning. FSU, when I attended, was a rigidly segregated entity in a rigidly segregated state. The only blacks allowed on campus came to cook, clean or tend the grounds. A regional meeting of the American Association of University Professors was moved at the administration's insistence when it was learned that African-American educators would be among those attending. A student from Florida A&M University who attempted to attend a concert in Opperman Music Hall that had been advertised as free and open to the public was expelled by security. For printing that story, *Florida Flambeau* editor Bruce Galphin endured a stern lecture from a dean. Though other southern universities had begun admitting blacks to their graduate programs under a Supreme Court decree that preceded public school desegregation, Florida was

Robert and Margaret Strozier in front of the president's house, 1957

stubbornly resistant. I was a freshman when the Brown decision foretold the end of school segregation in all respects. Though a substantial minority of FSU's students and faculty were ready and willing to comply, the Legislature was not. FSU's administration was of no mind to contest the racist politicians.

Only a year or so after Brown, however, the Interfraternity Council (IFC) threw tradition to the wind by signing Duke Ellington and his band for the Greeks' annual dance. This was big news, but before we could get it into the *Flambeau* there was a summons to the dean's office. The dean and the IFC president urged us to suppress the story. We weren't exactly forbidden, but they were leaning fairly hard. If the Legislature found out that blacks were coming to FSU in a professional capacity, to entertain Florida's precious white children, God alone knew what evil the politicians might do. Banning the dance might be only the beginning of it.

Privately, we knew they had a point. But to suppress a story as big as that? Then someone — I think it may have been the dean — had a brilliant idea. Print the story, he said. Just don't mention that Ellington and his band were black. By no means note that it was the first of anything.

That's what we did. The story appeared on page one of the *Flambeau*, at fair length under a modest headline. It mentioned that the Ellington band would also appear at Florida A&M, which was sharing the cost for its journey to Tallahassee. It did not say anything about anyone being Negro (the preferred term in those days). And of course there was no picture. So far as we knew, no one at the capitol took notice. We rationalized this self-censorship with the thought that, in a better world, it would be immaterial to what race the musicians belonged. Indeed, the only news value would be their indisputable artistic prominence.

And that is how it is today.

But I have never quite forgiven the Greeks for not inviting us to their dance.

"*I sincerely hope that the women of this campus will rally together in pursuit of female 'independen[ce.] twentieth century arrived quite a number of years ago. It should arrive soon at FSU.*"

CAY CRANFORD, 1958

Spring 1958: Bermuda Shorts, Swing, and Seminole Sports

On campus, '58 was a year of demand for change in women's rules. In April, Cay Cranford wrote that "FSU women's rules are mid-Victorian." She demanded "equal rights" for women students.

On May 10, for the first time, FSU coeds were permitted to wear Bermuda shorts on campus uncovered by raincoats. Dean of Women Katherine Warren, in making the announcement, stated: "We are confident that in enjoying the freedom and comfort of wearing Bermudas on Saturday on the campus women will continue to respect the place in which such attire is not appropriate. The wearing of short-shorts, slim-jims, pedal pushers, dungarees or slacks will not be permitted."

Florida State

1960: New President, New Coach, New Collection

"New" was the key word as the 1960 academic year opened at Florida State. FSU had a new president, Dr. Gordon W. Blackwell, and a new football coach, Bill Peterson. A new experiment in dorm living, the coed dorm, was opened in DeGraff Hall, and a new academic department, engineering science, was initiated.

The new football coach, whose speeches would in time become legendary, confined himself to talking about establishing a winning tradition at FSU.

The University Library received one of its most treasured gifts, the John M. Shaw Childhood in Poetry Collection. The more than 5,000 volumes have now grown to over 25,000. His family established an endowment fund to support the collection.

Florida State, 1978

Bob Miller (class of 1961): Memories

Honor Court, Men's Judiciary, Gold Key, Sigma Nu and the Famous Cowboy and Indian Party, Nick's Toggery, Silver Slipper, four years of ROTC, football games, tailgate parties, and being on the raiding party that delivered the famous Apalachicola anchor to the Delta Gamma sorority house . . . mysteriously.

Opposite top: 1958 snowfall on campus

Opposite bottom: President Emeritus Doak S. Campbell looks at a bust of himself, a gift of the class of 1958, done by Art Department faculty member Rudolph Jaegert.

Jim Apthorp (class of 1961): Memories of 1957 to 1961

After a thirty-year career in Florida government and the real estate business, Jim Apthorp returned to campus in 2000 to direct the Collins Center for Public Policy.

Several things stick in my mind about the time I spent as an undergraduate.

Race—No black students enrolled at FSU while I was here but there was much concern about the issue. During the summer of my sophomore year I attended a short discussion of race relations held at the University of Illinois under the sponsorship of the Field Foundation and the National Student Association. This was a truly transforming experience for me. It was the first time I had ever attended any meeting with blacks. My involvement with student government at FSU gave me this opportunity. As I look back on it, this brief experience changed me from a go-along southern student into a questioning southern adult for the rest of my life.

Kennedy-Nixon—The election of 1960 was the first one I could vote in. I found myself seriously divided from many friends and family members because of my support of John Kennedy. I've never been prouder of any vote. The campus atmosphere of questioning and debate helped me make that choice and gave me access to much of the information that formed its basis.

Maxwell Courtney, FSU's first African-American graduate, shaking the hand of President John Champion,1965.

Donn Dughi (class of 1962)

Donn Dughi has been covering Florida politics for almost forty years. He began as a reporter and photographer with WCTV in Tallahassee and in 1970 became photo bureau manager for United Press International (UPI). In 1988, the Florida House of Representatives passed a resolution honoring him for his unique coverage of the legislative process.

While at FSU I wrote several fictional and humorous pieces for the campus magazine *Smoke Signals* and studied creative writing under Pulitzer Prize–winner Michael Shaara. Another favorite English professor was Dr. Hudson Rogers, famous for his lectures on Robert Browning. It was said that some students were moved to tears when Rogers read from Browning's work. Rogers Hall is named for him.

I have recently retired as the official photographer for the Florida House of Representatives and live in Tallahassee, where I keep busy collecting old records, magazines, and campaign buttons. I'm also doing some creative writing, of which I'm sure my old friend and teacher, Mike Shaara, would have approved.

Cora Nell Spooner (class of 1967)

Bryan Hall was my dormitory of choice. I was an excited new freshman entering FSU in September 1962. Mama, Rebecca King (FSCW 1934), had lived there as a student, and Granell, Nellie Godfrey King (FFC 1906), had been Bryan's housemother. Bryan Hall is one of the oldest buildings on campus and was probably the least desirable living space.

I had played around the FSU campus as a child while Mama worked on another master's degree each summer. I, however, chose to room at Bryan, a home away from home.

I pledged Chi Omega in the fall of 1962. A little more than a year later my sisters and I gathered to watch the aftermath of President Kennedy's assassination on the TV in the family room of the XO house.

In 1964 the FSU football team defeated Florida for the first time. But then, there was the Vietnam war. . . . Life continues.

Michael Kasha, Professor of Chemistry, directed the operation of the Institute of Molecular Biophysics (IMB), begun in 1960 to study the application of chemical physics to molecular biology.

At the inauguration of Robert M. Strozier, President Emeritus Doak S. Campbell talks to (L to R) Arnold Greenfield, president of the student body; L.B. Vocelle, president of the Alumni Association; Governor LeRoy Collins and Professor of English William Hudson Rogers.

A gathering of Florida college and university presidents with FSU's Gordon W. Blackwell (1960–65). Seated, L to R: Henry King Stanford, University of Miami; William Kadel, Florida Presbyterian College; J. Ollie Edmunds, Stetson; Sister M. Dorothy, O.P., Barry College; J.B. Culpepper, Executive Director, Board of Control; J. Wayne Reitz, University of Florida; Kenneth R. Williams, Florida Atlantic University. Standing, L to R: Robert Spiro, Jacksonville University; Charles T. Thrift, Jr., Florida Southern College; George W. Gore, Jr., Florida A&M University; John S. Allen, University of South Florida; Edward J. McCarthy, Biscayne College; Gordon W. Blackwell, FSU; Harold B. Crosby, University of West Florida; David M. Delo, O.P., University of Tampa; Richard V. Moore, Bethune Cookman College; R.W. Puryear, Florida Memorial College; Myron R. Blee, Director, Florida Institute for Continuing University Studies.

**Karl Zerbe, a famed expressionist painter, taught at FSU until his
retirement in 1971. This is *Dancing Couple #1*, collage and acrylic on
canvas, 1961, permanent collection, LeMoyne Art Foundation.**

Nancy Smith Fichter (class of 1952, M.A. 1954), Professor
Emerita, Department of Dance

Nancy Smith Fichter chaired FSU's dance program for thirty-three years before retiring in 1997. In 2001 she was called back and named the interim dean of the School of Theatre.

Florida State University is woven into a very large part of the fabric of my life. I experienced it as a student (both undergraduate and master's degrees in English) and as a faculty member in dance. Although I left it for a while (to complete my doctoral work and to teach elsewhere), I returned in 1964 and stayed until retirement in 1997. The big dream was to build a place where serious dance could happen, a truly professional program that would send young dancers out into the world of concert dance and where the new dance could be made. It was the ideal of "the conservatory within the university," and that vision was beginning to be realized at a few places around the country in the 1950s and 1960s.

FSU has been the place to support that vision and today its dance program ranks among the top in the country. I will always be indebted to the place that has nurtured and supported the art that I serve. It certainly seemed like an unlikely alliance in those early days when there was considerable doubt expressed about the place for serious art-making in the groves of academe, but time has proved that the arts have a stellar role in a university and FSU has taken strong leadership in the arts.

My roots at FSU go way back. The first graduating class of Florida State College for Women was the class of 1910, and my mother was its president. Her name was Elise W. Partridge, and she was also the editor of the first yearbook, *Flastacowo.* Two of my sisters (Marianne D. Smith and Elise W. Smith) also attended this institution. So the genealogy is more than an institutional link!

Opposite: Nancy Smith (Fichter), third from left

Professor James P. Jones

James P. Jones, over forty years in the FSU history department, is a man of eclectic interests. Born and schooled in the Deep South, he has spent the greater part of his academic career chronicling Civil War-era Yankees. On another front he's become the recognized Boswell of Seminole gridiron feats and a major contributor to the FSU saga in basketball and baseball as well. First named to the Athletic Board in 1973, he served on selection committees that hired Bobby Bowden, Dick Howser, and Mike Martin, among others.

"You know, I went to school at the University of Florida and remained a Gator fan even after I began teaching at FSU," he says. "But one of my students in 1968 was quarterback Kim Hammond. When I saw a Gator player level him with a dirty hit during the game that year, I was so angry I spent the whole second half cheering for the Seminoles."

The best part of that story, Jones says, is that Hammond returned to throw a long touchdown pass to end Ron Sellers that won the game. And Jones's allegiance to the Garnet and Gold has never wavered since. Former students describe him as a "rigorous instructor" and a "dynamic classroom lecturer who knows how to make his subject come to life." C. Peter Ripley, who edited FSU's Black Abolitionist Papers project, calls him "easily one of the top teaching faculty members at this university." Ripley did his graduate work under Jones's tutelage, as did present FSU history professors Maxine Jones and Joe Richardson.

In 1957, still working on his doctorate, Jones jumped at an offer to join the FSU faculty as "temporary acting instructor of history." The pay was $4,000, he recalls, to teach world civilization and American survey. Even today, undergraduate classes remain a staple of his workload.

As a tribute to Jones's excellence in teaching, he has won, over three separate decades, the Coyle-Moore Award in 1962, President's Award in 1978, and a Distinguished Teaching Award in 1991. [In 1994 and 1996 Jones won the Teaching Incentive Award—TIP—and the University Teaching Award in 2002.] But distinguished research has also marked his career. Oddly enough, it was football that ignited his scholarly muse.

As Jones tells it, his first book chronicled the turbulent story of John A. "Blackjack" Logan, a Union general with strong political ambitions. After that, writer's block set in. "I couldn't come up with a thing," he says. "Finally, [FSU history professor] Bill Rogers asked me if I'd ever thought of doing a book on Seminole football." A regular at Seminole games and a favorite teacher of many Seminole players, Jones found that chronicling the team's early years came easily. It also broke his intellectual logjam.

In short order he went right into *Yankee Blitzkrieg: Wilson's Raid Through Alabama and Georgia* (1976), the story of Union General James Wilson's daring cavalry raid through Georgia and Alabama. First in longhand with a pencil, then rewriting on a manual typewriter, he's been churning out books and articles ever since. But it's still in the classroom where both Jones and his subjects best come to life. "This may sound hokey," he says. "But teaching is my greatest satisfaction. I love it. How many can truthfully say that?"

Andy Lindstrom, *Research in Review*, Winter 1995

Opposite top: Wiley and Lucilla Housewright, for whom the Wiley and Lucilla Housewright Chair in Music is named. Wiley Housewright was dean of the School of Music from 1966 to 1979.

Opposite left: Carlisle Floyd, the 1964–65 Robert O. Lawton Distinguished Professor, received the New York Music Critics award for his opera *Susannah*.

Opposite right: School of Music faculty (L to R) Owen Sellers, Thomas Wright, and Elena Nikolaidi in the sixties.

Hunt Hawkins is chairman of the Department of English.

In fall, the junior I wanted to be
practiced wheelies in the parking lot,
his gleaming blue Triumph absorbing every shock.
In winter, said the blond boy's poem,
the campus became an ashtray.
We had bunks in rooms meant for valets.
My roommate, a future dentist,
kept his desk lamp on night and day,
trying to sprout peas.
All he ever produced was a plate of dirt.
When Russian ships approached Cuba,
my classmates steamed off to the women's colleges,
convinced the world was about to end,
or at least hoping the girls would see it that way.
At our mixer, Bo Didley sang "I'm a Man."
Now I grow alarmed to find my class
sliding slowly forward in the Alumni magazine—
prospering, spawning, remarrying, whatever.
I can no longer remember most of them,
but I can still see the eyes
of the mother of the blond boy
when she asked us to be kind to him
because he was sicker than he knew.

Hunt Hawkins, *The Domestic Life*,
University of Pittsburgh Press, 1994

1963: Weejuns, Activism, and Black November

In the fall of 1963 Villager dresses and Weejuns were omnipresent among Florida State's 11,102 students (5,809 men and 5,293 women). Football was also very visible as Bill Peterson's men opened with a surprising 24–0 victory over Miami. In that game Fred Biletnikoff returned an interception 99 yards to score, establishing a record.

While much campus activity moved along familiar patterns, changes were nibbling at the fabric of traditional college life. "Activism" was a word heard with increasing frequency, and the cause gripping activists that autumn was integration. FSU students joined FAMU students in battling to integrate theaters and off-campus restaurants. Pro-integration pickets blocked the entrances to several spots on Copeland and Jefferson. Eventually five Florida State students were arrested as controversy raged across the university and through the Tallahassee community.

The event that most stunned the world in 1963 was President John F. Kennedy's assassination in Dallas on a black Thursday in November. On Friday, the *Flambeau* spoke for the university community when it said: "May God keep John Kennedy. May God have mercy on the soul of his assassin. And may God lead President Johnson and the United States through one of its blackest hours of sorrow and trouble."

Florida State

Scott Dailey (class of 1963)

Scott Daily is the executive director of the Florida Institute of Government.

I was a student at FSU in the early sixties. An interesting group of guys lived in the El Rancho neighborhood. All were older students, a few were married and a few, like myself, were veterans.

We loved to get out and toss the football around and play a game of "touch." One day, Larry Broer came home and announced that the Chemistry Department had organized a flag football team and wanted to challenge us. We won, and thus were born the El Rancho Chargers. We even beat the undefeated Geology Department. We entered the intramural flag football and came in second. Losing the tournament championship to, guess who, Geology.

We later entered teams in the basketball and softball tourneys. Late one evening at the "Tempo" it was decided that a couple of guys would enter the intramural tennis tournament the next day. Then came bowling. The El Rancho Chargers won the All Sports Trophy and, as was our nature, had a smashing good party to celebrate and brag.

As an FSU student, I worked at night for Avis Rent-a-Car at the airport. I frequently supplemented that income by shelving books at Strozier Library. I was hired by the library director, Miss Bethea, who had a no-nonsense reputation among her employees. If I had a particularly heavy class load, I would take a leave of absence knowing that she would always hire me back.

My shelving assignment was in Science and Technology on the third floor, east wing. This was not the job at the library I really wanted. I wanted to be the guy who sat at the front door and made sure that all library books were properly checked out. It was a great spot to meet people, especially female people. But I stayed on the third floor with kind, soft-spoken Mr. Myers, charmingly eccentric Miss Ezell, and the radiant and lovely Eloise Harbeson.

President Gordon Blackwell (L) and John Gabriel Kellum in 1963. Kellum was made business manager of Florida Female College in 1907 and retired in 1945 after thirty-eight successful and innovative years. Kellum Hall was named for him.

"When you're strange, no one remembers your name."

JIM MORRISON, POET/LEAD SINGER OF THE DOORS, FSU ATTENDEE 1962 AND 1963

Gideon R. Jones (1963–1993), Professor Emeritus, Special Education

The development of programs to prepare teachers and therapists for individuals with impairments is an important part of our university's work and history. While courses in special education existed before 1958—when Ellen Thiel arrived—it was she who brought structure and continuity to an assortment of courses in the Department of Psychology and the School of Education.

As the number of students and faculty increased, the program became a department in 1965. Under Dr. James Foshee's leadership as department head, expansion began.

Dr. L. L. Schendel followed James Foshee as department head. Larry Schendel was already highly respected by the faculty. Besides bringing to the department proven university administrative experience, he also brought programs in speech pathology and audiology, which had been stepchildren in the liberal arts Department of Speech.

The concept of preparing professionals, under a single university unit, to educate and rehabilitate people with impairments was so successful that many universities soon adapted similar administrative structures. Much of that success must go to L.L. Schendel.

Top: FSU campus, 1967,
west of Woodward Avenue

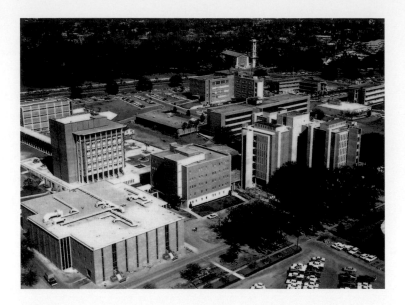

Martin Roeder (1964–1994), Professor Emeritus, Department of Biological Science

When I first came to FSU for an interview I had already known that in biology there was no place other than Tallahassee between Chapel Hill and New Orleans that I would have been interested in moving to. In January of 1964 I left North Carolina in a wool suit and lined trench coat to be greeted by 78 degree afternoons. The fact that my shirt was soaked was not due only to the stress of the interview process!

When I returned home I told my wife, Rae, my impression of the campus was that they were putting up a building in the middle of the library, such was the movement in all directions on the campus. It was only a couple of years later that a building was put up at the back end of the library! I was so impressed by the spirit of excitement on campus as it appeared that most everyone was busy at work but happy. When I joined the faculty later that year I entered into a collegial atmosphere where intellectual ferment was widespread and where the exchange of ideas was not limited to one's own discipline but crossed lines of specialties. Almost all the faculty were committed to making FSU a center for academic productivity and innovation.

Morton D. Winsberg (1963–1997), Professor Emeritus, Geography

You know you're getting older when the office building you watched being built is being remodeled because of age. I remember looking forward to moving into the new building, Bellamy, and leaving our antiquated temporary quarters.

Between 1965, when I arrived, and 1970, the Department of Geography was housed in the basement of Dodd Hall. Our offices were cooled by window air conditioners with condensation leaking over the floor. Two professors to an office, we did our research and met our students. Instruction was in basement rooms nearby, most without windows.

In those days the Department of Hotel and Restaurant Management was housed in what is today called Johnston Hall, as was the Department of Anthropology. Restaurant management required its students to organize and produce a meal, the choice of presentation and cuisine being theirs. Since Tallahassee restaurants were rather limited (I don't think the town had even a Chinese restaurant), many looked forward to these modestly priced, "haute cuisine" meals.

As one would expect, the success of a meal varied greatly according to the students' skill and enthusiasm. During one meal featuring Hawaiian cuisine, a tiki torch set palm leaves on fire and the room had to be evacuated. Another time a student prepared an elaborate dessert flambé on a trolley next to some diners. Evidently he applied too much liquor. When he lit the dessert, the flame leaped out of control. The student jumped backward, upset the trolley, and blue flames spread under the table.

Also, Anthropology students delighted in disrupting these dinners and once released a live monkey into the dining room. The monkey, ordinarily used for demonstrations in physical anthropology classes, caused chaos.

Today the university has many more students than in the 1960s, and its faculty is much more research oriented. Both students and faculty can take advantage of an infrastructure that a sixties faculty member could not have imagined. Nonetheless, certain delightful elements of that decade have been eroded and even lost.

Perhaps I romanticize the past more than I ought, but I feel it was a period of great collegiality and gentility, both among the faculty and the students.

In early September 1965, slightly more than 13,000 students arrived in Tallahassee to begin the fall trimester at Florida State University. Two hundred of those students were foreign, a new university record. In addition, 199 exceptional freshmen students joined the Honors Program, directed by Dr. Paul Piccard, Political Science.

A new building, Rogers Hall, an apartment-style dorm built to house graduate students, was dedicated as the academic year opened. In the ceremony Dr. Doak Campbell and President John Champion paid tribute to the man for whom it was named, Dr. William Hudson Rogers, a longtime popular English professor. Florida Hall, a woman's dorm, was renamed Deviney Hall in honor of former zoology professor Ezda May Deviney.

Two items of interest to male students appeared in the *Flambeau* that September. Nic's Toggery offered the almost mandatory Bass Weejuns for $13 and the paper carried draft news.

The year's cultural offerings opened with the brilliant French mime Marcel Marceau, soon to be followed by the Harkness Ballet.

Following the great FSU grid success of 1964, hopes were high as the '65 season opened. Coach Bill Peterson's men opened against Texas Christian University but fell 7–3. Baylor came to town next and FSU bounced back 9–7. The third clash saw FSU drop a narrow loss 26–24 to Kentucky. That night, however, a dormant tribe offense came alive. The biggest play saw two old Daytona High School friends, T.K. Wetherell and Bill Moreman, combine on a 100-yard touchdown on a kick return.

One week later Pete's gridders bounced back 10–3 to upset the nationally ranked Georgia Bulldogs. Then came Alabama and VPI. The Tide crushed FSU 21–0, but the Garnet and Gold fought back to edge the Gobblers 7–6. On the weekend that FSU lost to Alabama, some good news came from Gainesville. The FSU frosh defeated the Gator frosh 13–7. Leading the Seminole yearlings were two Jacksonville athletes named Gary Pajcic and Ron Sellers.

Florida State's seventh game in 1965 was homecoming and the opponent the Wake Forest Demon Deacons. Major homecoming entertainment came from folk singers Peter, Paul and Mary, then at their peak. A sellout crowd in Tully Gym roared with applause in spite of the acoustics.

On this beautiful fall weekend in the mid-sixties the campus stood at a dividing point. With one foot in the traditional campus life of the past, 1965 saw FSU and most American universities look toward a new and troubled era. Much of the trouble had already gripped the nation, but for Florida State University racial tensions and the strife over the war in Vietnam were things of the future. Sitting in Tully Gym listening to Peter, Paul and Mary sing "Blowin' in the Wind," you could feel that future moving ever closer.

Florida State, Summer 1979

Opposite top: FSU's first Nobel Prize winner, chemist Robert S. Mulliken, with Mary Champion at a congratulatory dinner in his honor.
Opposite bottom: Marcel Marceau at FSU for the Artist Series, c.1964. Pictured (L to R): Pierre Vervy, Marcel Marceau and Dick Puckett. Ralph Hurst did the large figure of Marceau's character BIP.

Barbara Amman (class of 1967)

Barbara Amman received a degree in education from FSU and returned for a law degree (1996). She currently practices law in Tallahassee.

Picture it: the evening of check-in day at Jennie Murphree Hall, Florida State University, early fall 1966; the parlor of the all-girls dorm; a room full of freshmen women.

I was a member of the group. The House Mother introduced herself and told us we were the Jennie Murphree "roses." She was ahead of her time, for the central theme of her lecture was "Just say no!"—to everything. In 1966, FSU representatives boasted to freshmen that the faculty and staff took their "in loco parentis" role seriously.

During her speech, the House Mother held high a long-stemmed red rose—telling us we were all united under that symbol and its beauty. She handed the rose to a girl with the instruction that we were each to touch and pass the rose to every young woman seated in the parlor.

While we silently passed the rose, she went on without pause about Jennie Murphree rules. One rule still stands out: We were to meet our "gentlemen callers," if we had any, only in the parlor. No men were permitted beyond the parlor's vestibule, which held the receptionist's booth. The receptionist, during the acceptable times only, would page us in our rooms were it our good fortune to have a gentleman caller.

At that first meeting, the House Mother talked on and on. As we shifted restlessly, hoping for an ending, the rose continued to circulate among us "roses." Finally, the last person passed the rose to the House Mother. The rose was certainly not its former beautiful self. She held it high and concluded her speech full of admonitions with one last one: "Girls, look closely at this rose. This is what happens when a Jennie Murphree Rose is handled!"

J. Sid Raehn (class of 1969):The Silent Majority

In 1968 the war in Vietnam was raging. Students across the country were rebelling against the war. The Florida Legislature, in protest of the protests, had just voted down a major educational bond issue that would have infused much-needed cash into the university system. Gallop announced a report that only 2% of college students were involved in campus unrest.

That's why two undergrads, at 2 a.m. in the morning, called Dr. Marshall at home. They had an idea. At 2:15 they were drinking milk and eating chocolate chip cookies at the table in his kitchen. I was one of the two. I wanted to use the Gallop poll to change the public mindset that all students were rebelling against the war and were involved in administrative disruption and violence.

I wanted to circulate a petition among students, starting with those at Florida State, that basically said, "We are the majority and we are not involved. We choose no longer to remain silent." I gave the movement a name, the Silent Majority. The phrase had never been used before; I coined it at 3 a.m. in President Marshall's kitchen. This quickly gained national attention. Eventually, CBS came to Tallahassee to film our group and its activities. Walter Cronkite aired the group and reported its purpose. Telegrams from all over the world, from the U.S. Senate and House, and from the office of the president, flooded FSU. President Nixon invited me and the co-chair, John Gerhime, to meet with him in Key Biscayne. Nixon asked us if he could use our phrase, the silent majority, in his upcoming State of the Union address. Permission was granted. The rest is history.

When I came to FSU on a football scholarship in 1966, there were no African Americans on the football team. The first black football player came to FSU in 1968. His name was Calvin Patterson. Patterson was from Miami Palmetto High School, where as a sophomore he was a starter on his high school team. This itself was no easy feat, since he was also one of the first blacks to break the color barrier at his high school.

Calvin and I became very good friends at FSU. In fact, we were roommates in the football dorm for a year. Calvin was a special person in many ways. He was smart, witty, sensitive, personable, and an exceptional athlete. But his life at FSU was no picnic. Like many black persons who were the "first," he experienced indignities, hostility, and even personal threats while breaking the color barrier. And he did it all by himself. For one full year he was the *only* black on the team. He persevered in the face of these conditions and did not quit.

After Patterson led the way in 1968, five more African Americans attended FSU the following year. Most of those five had very successful careers at FSU and some even went on to play pro ball. Patterson, for various reasons, never played a down of varsity ball at FSU, but his role in beginning what has become a long tradition of gifted black football players at FSU should not be forgotten.

Calvin helped me to broaden my outlook at a crucial point in my life. He helped me to understand what it was like to be black in the South in the late 1960s and early 1970s and to put life experiences in their proper perspective.

It is unfortunate, and terribly sad, that Patterson did not live long enough to see and appreciate the full extent of what he began in 1968. He died a tragic death in 1972 at the age of twenty-two. Although his name does not appear in any FSU record books, his role in FSU football history is a significant one. FSU fans and players owe him recognition and thanks.

Florida State ®

ROBERT URICH

Robert Urich, 1946–2002 (class of 1968)

He played tough-but-compassionate detectives, sensitive wanderers and romantic heroes. But Robert Urich, who died April 16, was best remembered in Tallahassee as Florida State's "other famous football-playing actor."

Like the more celebrated Burt Reynolds, Urich came to FSU as a highly touted football star whose athletic career ended in injury. Like Reynolds, Urich turned to acting and became a star of television and movies. And, like Reynolds, Urich never lost his affection for FSU.

In 1996, Urich was one of ten former football players who pledged $50,000 to help build the FSU Varsity Club at Campbell Stadium. In 1998, he taped a popular promotional ad for the university, thanking former teachers and touting the benefits of an FSU education. He was a frequent spectator at FSU games and never failed to mention his FSU background to interviewers.

He was most renowned for playing detectives in two series, *Vega$* and *Spenser: For Hire*. In the 1980s and 1990s, Urich earned critical acclaim for roles in several miniseries and television movies, most notably the Emmy–award-winning *Lonesome Dove*.

Urich's affection for his alma mater extended to the FSU School of Theatre. In 1980, he spent a weekend talking to FSU students putting on a production of *The Rainmaker*. In the late 1980s, he turned to retired theatre dean Richard Fallon for assistance in getting a play produced at Washington's Kennedy Center.

In fact, Urich's first acting experience was in a student production of *The Cavedwellers*. "Back then, football players looking for easy credits would take my stagecraft class because they got credit for working backstage," Fallon said. "Bob decided to try out."

Gerald Ensley, *Tallahassee Democrat,* April 17, 2002

Freestylers Seeley Feldmeyer and Bob Bell, 1967

FSU golf team, 1967. Hubert M. Green, fifth from left, is ranked 15th on the Senior PGA tour. Green won the 1977 U.S. Open Championship and the 1985 PGA Championship.

1965 Seminole defense: the Seven Magnificents and their backfield

Lawrence Cunningham (M.A. 1963, Ph.D. 1969)

In the late 1960s I got my Ph.D. in humanities but had already joined the Religion Department as an instructor. Except for a stint in Florence, Italy, and a year as a visiting professor in Pennsylvania, I remained on the faculty, climbing through the ranks from assistant to full professor.

In 1987 I decided to leave the lush joys of Florida for the more austere pleasures of northern Indiana. I am now completing my fourteenth year at the University of Notre Dame, where, a few months ago, I was installed as the John O'Brien Professor of Theology.

I could never begin to name the friends and colleagues and students who sustained me in my years at Florida State. Many, newly recruited to the university, would regularly complain of being in the north Florida boondocks, but curiously enough, it is the environs of Tallahassee that I most fondly remember. I love the South and have a particular fondness for azaleas, long leaf pines, Bradley's ground grits, fishing at the Dog Island reef, and bird watching at the Saint Mark's Wildlife Preserve. I loved walking in the old Betton Hills neighborhood where I once lived, on the lookout for the rufous-sided towhee that used to hang out up the road. I loved eating seafood on the coast, taking particular pleasure in the knowledge that we were hundreds of miles from any city worthy of the name.

So why did I leave to go to Notre Dame? When I told my then chairman, Walter A. Moore, that I had decided to take this new job, he said, "Well, you are a scholar—interested in Catholicism—and getting an offer from Notre Dame is like Jesus calling you back to heaven."

It is heavenly, but I have discovered a few things about this earthly paradise. It is very hard to find decent grits, it is a long way to the Gulf of Mexico, and the winters are penitential.

Edward T. Johnson, Jr. (class of 1968)

Voice was my instrument; I was a music education major. Though I received voice lessons only from graduate assistants, with the exception of David Wingate in my senior year, I got very good training from them.

The most outstanding professor at FSU for me was Dr. John Fenton Spratt, born in 1917. I first had Dr. Spratt in the basic music history course in fall of 1965, held in the choir room. He frequently had his pipe in his mouth (between tampings and relightings) as he would explain phenomena of music history, how they related to history, literature, philosophy, and to each other.

My memories of Florida State are priceless. Over 17,000 baby boomers joined me during that window of time, flung together on a few hundred northern Florida acres for education, socialization, and career training. These were years in a time of national transition, years of considerable influence, and years in our lives that we all wish in retrospect we could live—at least parts of—over again.

But never to be lost are my many happy memories of my first alma mater, a great university, and its great Music School. FSU's impact upon my life has been great, and I will always be grateful for the opportunities for growth it offered me.

In 1969 a fire thought to have started on the fourth floor did serious damage to
Westcott. It took several years for the building to be completely restored.

John E. Champion (1956–1985), Professor Emeritus, Accounting;
President, 1965–1968

There were many wonderful experiences for me during my years at FSU. I had an opportunity as a faculty member to serve on practically every major university committee, as an administrator to deal with fiscal and physical aspects of the school, and finally, as president, to work on the goals and objectives of the university.

As associate dean of the College of Business, I and Dean Charles A. Rovetta worked successfully to gain full accreditation for the college in the national Collegiate Schools of Business. As vice-president of administration I was so proud to be a part of the tremendous growth, almost like an explosion, of campus building. When I ride around campus and see the Fine Arts Building, the physics, chemistry, infirmary, and law school buildings, I think, "Well, I had a small part in their development." The first law school class, under Dean Mason Ladd, was amazing. One hundred percent of the graduates passed the Florida Bar examination when they took it.

I can never forget the excitement on campus when it was announced that Dr. Robert Mulliken, an FSU professor of chemical physics, had won the Nobel Prize, a first for the state. We had a tremendous School of Music and a wonderful theatre program. I'll never forget the time that Pablo Casals came to FSU and the honorary degree that we gave the great classical guitarist Andrés Segovia. I think about the exciting programs given by our own faculty, about sitting in an auditorium packed with students, faculty, and townspeople to hear the performances of Kilenyi and Dohnányi.

In 1968 Florida State was named one of thirty Centers of Excellence in the country by the National Science Foundation. I think of my excitement when members of our faculty were elected to the Academy of Science; I respect the contributions our scientists have made and continue to make. I'm proud of our center in Florence, Italy, and how the first group studying abroad helped to save art objects during a flood. The Italian government gave them an honor for their actions. I'm proud of the FSU Circus, an internationally outstanding extracurricular activity. I think about our baseball program and the many outstanding young men who have gone out as coaches and leaders.

Looking back now it gives me a great deal of satisfaction to have had the opportunity to be a part of this great university. I feel as though I have truly "grown up" with Florida State.

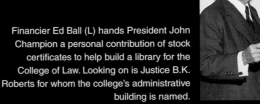

Financier Ed Ball (L) hands President John Champion a personal contribution of stock certificates to help build a library for the College of Law. Looking on is Justice B.K. Roberts for whom the college's administrative building is named.

"Looking back now it gives me a great deal of satisfaction to have had the opportunity to be a part of this great university. I feel as though I have truly 'grown up' with Florida State."

PRESIDENT JOHN E. CHAMPION

Top: Baseball player Ted Williams, in town at the invitation of FSU's Athletic Department, visits with President John Champion.

Bottom: (L to R) President John Champion, wife Mary and Governor Claude Kirk

PRESIDENTS **STANLEY MARSHALL** (1969–1976),
BERNARD F. SLIGER (1977–1991),
DALE LICK (1991–1993)

CHANGE

The close of the 1960s witnessed an extraordinary strengthening of the university's stature and resources, a new strengthening that became permanent over the next quarter-century. In many ways, a 1968 National Science Foundation seed grant of $4.8 million signaled Florida State's arrival in science training and research. Jump forward to 1990, when the same foundation awarded FSU the National High Magnetic Field Laboratory—and Nobel Laureate John Schrieffer agreed to be its chief scientist. ¶ Nor was FSU's eminence restricted to the sciences. English professor Michael Shaara won the 1975 Pulitzer Prize for his novel *The Killer Angels*. In 1976 Bobby Bowden became FSU's seventh football coach, and the same year an accomplished undergraduate, Carolyn Alexander, was named the school's first Rhodes Scholar. ¶ Her achievement was one of many FSU firsts for women and other groups, mirroring America's struggle for diversity. In 1976 Dobie Flowers was crowned the Seminoles' first black homecoming queen. A year later President Bernard Sliger named Dr. Bob Leach the vice-president for student affairs, making him FSU's first African American vice-president. In 1985 FSU created one of its most prestigious honors, the Martin Luther King, Jr., Distinguished Service Award. During this period too, an FSU alumna, Barbara Palmer (class of 1970), re-turned as women's athletic director—a response to the federal Title IX mandate of equality for women in sports. ¶ These particular events unfolded within an overall transformation of FSU's academic and financial structures spearheaded by three presidents: Stanley Marshall, Bernard (Bernie) Sliger, and Dale Lick.

President Stanley Marshall

President Bernard F. Sliger

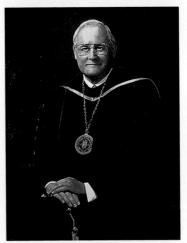

President Dale Lick

Opposite: Sue Braswell speaking for
Students for a Democratic Society,
March 4, 1969

TAP030403-3/4/69-TALLAHASSEE,FLA.: Sue Braswell of Cocoa Beach, a spokesman for Students for a Democratic Society, discusses what action SDS should take if Fred Gordon, a national SDS officer is refused a hall to speak on the Florida State Campus tonight. UPI TELF dd/dd

Vietnam, Cambodia, Kent State, moratorium, and *demonstration* were words sweeping campus in the spring of 1970. Florida State, like most major American universities, was in the grip of intense student unrest, unparalleled in the history of higher education. On April 14 an antiwar rally called for "immediate and total withdrawal from Vietnam," and 350 FSU and FAMU students marched on the capitol.

Three weeks later U.S. forces invaded Cambodia, the Kent State students were killed, and FSU swirled with protests. Students marched on the governor's mansion and then across campus to the ROTC building shouting, "ROTC must go—now!" Drill was called off because of tension on campus. On May 6 an all-night vigil on Westcott lawn followed a brief takeover of the administration building.

Over the next two days the demonstrations reached a crescendo. Fifteen hundred students ringed the ROTC building, causing minor conflicts with the police. On May 8, classes were suspended to demonstrate "concern and sorrow" for the Kent State students. That night Governor Claude Kirk came to the university, sat in a chair on Landis Green, and spent a long time talking to students.

Other campus changes were evidence of 1970's turbulent spring. CPE (Center for Participant Education) began its career, enrolling 150 students in such new-departure courses as Women, Photojournalism, The Hippie and Society, Chess, and Astrology. Ecologists proclaimed the first Earth Day on April 22, celebrated at FSU with special programs about the embattled environment.

One last transformation from FSCW to FSU occurred on May 26. The administration announced the abolition of all curfews for women students. Finally men and women were treated equally (in curfews, at least).

On a campus whose most obvious feature seemed to be change, one area was remarkably the same: athletics. In many ways the spring of 1970 was FSU's finest to date in intercollegiate sports. Dave Cowens ended a brilliant hoop career and was drafted by the Boston Celtics. Future olympic diving champion Phil Boggs finished second in the NCAA. The track team, led by Ken Misner, shipped the Gators 85–60. Most successful of all was the Florida State baseball team, ranked first nationally for the season's final month until edged by one run by Southern Cal in the NCAA final.

"WE DON'T WANT ANY!"

Top: Doug Marlette, an FSU alum, worked on the *Florida Flambeau* as a student. The Pulitzer Prize–winning cartoonist joined the staff of the *Tallahassee Democrat* as their editorial cartoonist in July 2002.

Opposite: Comedian/activist Dick Gregory arriving in Tallahassee in 1969 to perform

"*1968, the year I arrived on campus as a clueless freshman, marked the dividing line between then and now in American history. It had a lasting—even chilling—effect on the world. And now I realize that it had a profound impact on me, shaping values and views I would carry into FSU student government, values and views I hold equally important now.*"

Marshall Criser, chancellor of the Board of Regents, called a meeting with Stan Marshall, Lou Hill, and several others. It was December 27, 1972, and he told us that the Athletic Department was $600,000 in debt. If we didn't raise some money by June 30, serious cutbacks were coming.

We put our heads together, raised the money, and formed what is now known as the Seminole Boosters. We continued to raise money, had a great time doing it, and shortly thereafter decided we needed some big givers. Thinking that big was $5,000 a year, we founded the Golden Chiefs. Silver Chiefs gave $2,500; the next level down, $500 or less. We wanted to provide parking for the Golden Chiefs, nice gold jackets, and two tickets to sit in the president's box.

Dale Lick appointed me as chairman of the first FSU Foundation Capital Campaign sometime around 1993. This was a chance to raise money for the academic side of the university rather than the Athletic Department. We made a few trips up to Atlanta and other places to call on people and get the campaign going. By the time Sandy D'Alemberte came, we had the Capital Campaign going and were delighted with its success to that point.

One of FSU's very good friends, and a wonderful family friend of mine, was Marguerite Neal Williams from Thomasville, Georgia. She had been on the A-team to help raise the money for the stadium. Well, she also gave, in segments, the first million for the Capital Campaign. When we reached our $200 million goal, Sandy and the trustees for the foundation extended it to $250 million. Well, we got to $250 million, and then we said, "Let's go to $300 million." Soon we had received $299 million.

Just before we were to play Florida in the Sugar Bowl for the national championship, my wife Marian and I went up to Thomasville, took Marguerite out to lunch, and asked her for the final million to make it $300 million. She said, "Well, I'm sorry George, I can't do it."

So we had lunch, parted, and then my wife and I went to the Sugar Bowl. Some time later (unfortunately, FSU lost), we returned to the hotel room and saw the red light on the phone flashing. It was a message from Marguerite to call her in Thomasville. She said, "George, I am going to give you that last million dollars to make it $300 million." What a gem of a person! We will always appreciate so much what she did for FSU.

Top: George Langford, 1990

Bottom: Rep. Talbot D'Alemberte, 1969

Opposite top: Alice Chambers at a 1970 retirement party in her honor, surrounded by former employers. From L: former commissioner of education Colin English, former president Doak Campbell, President Stanley Marshall, and former president John Champion.

Opposite bottom: Michael Shaara (L), member of the English Department faculty from 1959 to 1973, with President Stanley Marshall (center) and Arts and Sciences dean Robert Spivey upon Shaara's being awarded the Pulitzer Prize for fiction for his Civil War novel, *The Killer Angels*, in 1975.

I: Until 1962, no black student had enrolled at Florida State University. Many at the university knew it was time, and the opportunity presented itself in the form of a summer institute for junior high school science teachers sponsored by the Department of Science Education in the College of Education. I then served as department head.

I had applied to the National Science Foundation for support for teachers from Broward County to learn the latest methods in teaching junior high school science. Our proposal was approved in March, as I recall, and we had until June to prepare for the institute and especially for the racial integration of the university.

President Gordon Blackwell was determined that the academic program would proceed and that the black students would find the campus hospitable. Of course, none of us could predict how the black students would be received. Memories of the troubles in Alabama were fresh, and the apprehension of university officials was unmistakable.

Nor did we know what position the *Tallahassee Democrat* would take. The editor was Malcolm Johnson, a well-known conservative columnist whose views, until that time, were thought to be in harmony with the segregationists elsewhere in the South.

In the weeks before the institute, President Blackwell conducted a number of planning meetings in his office. Attending were the top administrative officers, along with representatives of the Leon County Sheriff's Department, Tallahassee Police Department, and state law enforcement, and—due to President Blackwell's foresight—Malcolm Johnson. Mr. Johnson attended all of the meetings and sat quietly at the end of the table taking notes and saying nothing. Mr. Johnson was well regarded in the Tallahassee community, especially by "old Tallahassee," which included the city and county commissions, most members of the Legislature, and much of the North Florida power structure. At the same time, those of us acquainted with Mr. Johnson knew him to be a person of integrity who would give considerable weight to the welfare of the university and the community. Nonetheless, we waited expectantly for his piece in the newspaper.

We found it there on Monday morning, the day classes began. It was titled, "Education, Not Agitation," and Mr. Johnson laid out the case clearly. It was time, he said, to proceed with education for students of all creeds and colors and that he had observed the students (who had arrived over the weekend) to be here for an education, not agitation.

Those of us involved in the institute believed that Malcolm Johnson's editorial did much to allow us to integrate the university peacefully and to smooth the way for the full-time students who enrolled at FSU two years later.

II: From about 1969 to 1972, activists on campus were intent on a symbolic closing of the university, as had been done at many other universities. The protesters were pressing for a day's shutdown, or even for a few periods. The symbolism was important to me, too, but I was determined that the university would not close nor would classes be canceled even for a period. I felt the protesters' real goal was to challenge the administration's authority; any victory would have encouraged further efforts.

So, in May 1970, shortly after the tragic loss of lives on the Kent State and Jackson State University campuses, members of the Faculty Senate Steering Committee asked for a special meeting of the senate to discuss the protesters' requests. As the senate's presiding officer, I agreed. Other faculty members and students were expected to attend so the meeting was scheduled for Ruby Diamond at four o'clock on a Friday afternoon.

When I entered the auditorium at a few minutes before four, I found the auditorium filled. As I turned to face the crowd and call the meeting to order, I saw a large Vietcong flag hanging from the balcony. I asked that it be removed before the meeting was called to order. No movement was made to remove the flag, and I decided to seek the counsel of the university's vice-presidents, seated in the front row of seats.

This was a hot May afternoon, and as I faced the audience in un-air-conditioned Ruby Diamond, I saw a group of tense, sweaty faces and, scattered throughout the auditorium, young people (some of whom were not students) who seemed ready for a more active protest. I remembered police reports of ammunition purchases at Tallahassee gun shops and, for the first time, felt the possibility of physical violence.

While we waited for the flag to be removed, I walked over to Cecil Mackey, the executive vice-president, and whispered, "What do you think, Cecil?" He peered back over his shoulder and replied, "I think I'd go ahead with the meeting." Two other vice-presidents seated nearby agreed. I walked back to the rostrum feeling that I would probably protest but go ahead with the meeting.

As I turned to face the audience and saw the Vietcong flag, I just couldn't do it. I decided to appeal once again to the protesters. I explained that we had sent messages of condolence to the other universities, that closing FSU would do nothing to help the victims or their loved ones or to bring peace to those campuses; that while Vietnam was not our enemy in the formal diplomatic sense, the situation there was a national tragedy; and that I believed the taxpayers of Florida, who were supporting our university, would not approve of my conducting a meeting of an official university body with that banner prominently displayed. I said that I would wait three minutes for the flag to be removed—but I didn't say what would happen if it were not.

In a minute or so, the hands on the flagpole began to turn and the flag was rolled up. Of course, I would have had no choice but to refuse to call the meeting to order if it had not been removed. I would have beckoned my staff to follow me as we left—or attempted to leave—the auditorium. No one can say what would have happened then, but the incident stands out as the tensest moment during a tense period.

Shirley Marshall: An Adventure

In the early seventies, a time of student unrest nationwide, Stan and I were at a banquet when Stan's beeper went off. Chief Bill Tanner of the FSU campus police needed him. He was concerned because a group belonging to Students for a Democratic Society were marching to the president's home and seemed to be in an ugly mood. We had four of our five children living at home with us, aged two to sixteen, and Chief Tanner assured us that they had been taken to a friend's house and were fine. He did, however, want Stan to speak with the students from the front porch.

After we arrived, about forty students soon appeared. All of the outside lights were on. Chief Tanner told the students that President Marshall was there to talk to them. Initially there was a lot of yelling and the situation seemed volatile, but after about thirty minutes with Stan they departed without incident. We felt we had done the best we could. Still, we left our children at the friends' home for the night, not knowing if the students might come back.

The next morning we discovered that the bricks outlining a large flower bed across from the front porch were in disarray. Chief Tanner told us that his men had seen students holding bricks behind their backs. We knew of situations on other campuses where bricks were thrown, fires started, etc., and so we were grateful that our students had behaved so well in response to Stan's meeting with them.

L to R: Actress Helen Hayes and her brother-in-law John McArthur talk to President Stanley Marshall and his wife Shirley, early 1970s.

Opposite top: Bob Hope rehearsing in Tully Gym, 1972

Opposite bottom: Lotte Lenya in town for a 1972 Florida State University production of *Threepenny Opera*

Lenya's Back in Town

Lotte Lenya is in town for a Florida State University production of *Threepenny Opera*. Here to recreate her role of Jenny Diver, the wistfully treacherous little whore who betrays her lover MacHeath to the police, Lenya says with an impish twinkle, "Jenny hasn't changed—she's still a two-bucks girl—I'm just a little older."

    Threepenny Opera became a legendary success when it opened in Berlin in 1928 not only for its Vienna born star, Lenya, but for the author Bertolt Brecht and for the man who wrote the music, Kurt Weill, Lenya's husband for twenty-four years until his death in 1950.

Mary Ann Lindley, excerpted from the *Tallahassee Democrat*, April 9, 1972

Richard G. Fallon (1957–1989), Dean Emeritus and Professor,
School of Theatre

*Richard Fallon, admirably served FSU's theatre program from 1957
to 1989.*

A *Miami Herald* columnist once said FSU's Asolo Theatre company in
Sarasota had the "daring of a cat burglar." This could describe the
theatre program at FSU since 1957.

A good example took place during the opening of the Fine Arts
Building in 1971. Originally the departments of art and speech were to
be moved into the new building, but it soon became clear that both
would not fit. So, Dr. Robert Lawton, then dean of arts and sciences,
decided to separate theatre from the speech department, creating a
new department which I would chair.

Around that time a good friend of mine, Chandler Cowles, came to
see our new setup. He was a flamboyant rancher, theatre producer,
and prime supporter of Italy's Spoleto Festival of Two Worlds. Cowles
proposed inviting Gian Carlo Menotti, the distinguished Italian
composer (also trained in the United States), to direct his first
nonoperatic play, *The Leper*, here. The FSU administration was
thrilled. Menotti accepted and brought two professional actors with
him. This became big news throughout the state and country. We
decided to ask Menotti if he might invite some of the international
celebrities who followed him everywhere and he agreed.

Word leaked out that Greta Garbo had accepted and might make a
rare appearance. This was only the beginning. As the list grew so did
Cowle's concern that this celebrated group should not have to make
their own way to Tallahassee. I approached president Stanley Marshall
and suggested that FSU charter a plane to pick up the celebrities in
New York as well as return them after the premiere. He agreed.

I was commuting regularly to Sarasota because of the Asolo
Theatre. While at the airport I got a call from President Marshall. He
had one day to cancel the charter without incurring cost and wanted
to make sure enough celebrities were coming to warrant the plane.
Telephoning Cowles, I found that we had only four firm acceptances.
Despite a terrible sinking feeling, I told Marshall to go ahead with
the charter.

I had recruited about seventy-five members of the community to
contribute one hundred dollars each for the honor of meeting the
celebrities and to help pay for their housing and entertainment.
This group, plus the president, Cowles, Mennotti, and I, gathered at
a luncheon and waited to greet the plane. We had no word whether
the plane had actually left New York, not to mention how many
people were onboard. The president kept eyeing me, and I realized
I was as white as a sheet. Finally the group arrived: ninety of the
most illustrious celebrities ever to appear in Tallahassee. These
included the first-string theatre critic from the *New York Times*,
who gave FSU its first *Times* review; the pretender to the Italian
throne; the Italian ambassador; distinguished poets, composers,
and actors, including Tony Randall; and many very wealthy people
interested in the arts. When it was all over, we had raised money
for the school, the School of Music was invited to Spoleto, and
many lasting friendships were forged.

William Saroyan (L) at a reception for his play at FSU in the '70s, with Mart Hill,
of the theatre patron's group, and Dean Richard G. Fallon

"I already knew I wanted to be a meteorologist—all four of us Pfost boys from Dunedin graduated from FSU. My first visit to the FSU campus was in the mid-60s. I also remember a blind streaker with his cane."

RUSSELL PFOST (CLASS OF 1977)

Bucky McMahon: Streaking

Bucky McMahon completed a Ph.D. in English at FSU in 1992. He is a correspondent for Outside *magazine and a contributing editor for* Esquire.

I was hovering at my desk in a caffeine/amphetamine/finals-week fugue state trying to fit great square pegs of Freshman World History into the round holes of my hugely dilated pupils when I felt the earth outside Magnolia Hall begin to tremble. Earthquake? There were shouts in the dorm hallway, doors banging, footfalls pounding away in all directions at once; a sort of panic. The door clapped open and my neighbor George Bagley stuck his long-haired, granny-glasses-wearing, hippy-fied head in and said, "Streakers!"

Damn the Ancients; here was contemporary history happening right outside the dorm. At least it looked impressive, a throng thousands strong gathered on Landis Green on a fine spring night, all naked in moonlight. Whatever impetus had chased them here beside the fountain on the slope above Strozier Library had momentarily dissipated, and they entered into a panting, milling phase, eyes grazing, as it were, upon each other's bare nakedness in amazement,

nobody going anywhere. I kicked off my flip-flops, whipped off my tee-shirt, stepped out of my gym shorts, and blended in. Once among the sea of skin, it wasn't Them anymore but Us; We the Nude. And then we began to move.

I'd seen it a bunch of times on nature shows, how the sentinel zebra's head snaps up from the grass; it sniffs the lion and is off like a streak, every other damn zebra behind that executive decision a hundred and ten per cent. But I'd never personally been in a stampede before, nor have I since. The pleasure is greatly underrated.

On Landis Green that night you couldn't tell who the leaders were, what spooked them into action, or where they meant to take us, and least of all why. Nervous motion rippled through the ranks in waves. In one giant moonlit body we wheeled uphill, facing south toward Jefferson Street, and fell in behind the behind in front of us. We started out tight-packed at a jog-trot and then stretched out to a hard, joyous run, hair flying, nostrils flaring, bouncing, jiggling. Naked! All of us! At last! At last! You could hear above the chuff of heaving breaths a constant silly whinnying, hilarity fueling the herd. It was 1974 and we were so young, and so healthy, that it must have just plain hurt.

Theodore P. Williams (1966–2000), Professor Emeritus, Department of Biological Science

Ted Williams, a biologist and creative writer, came to Florida State in 1966 as a faculty member in Biological Science with a joint appointment at the Institute of Molecular Biophysics (IMB). With an interest in psychobiology/neuroscience he assumed the directorship of IMB from 1984–1990. He started the current program in structural biology and in 1991 moved to the Biomedical Research Facility. An expert in the photochemical processes of vision related to human sight, he retired in 2000.

Hale G. Smith, founder of FSU's Department of Anthropology (L) and Robert C. Dailey, Anthropology, study human remains in the Forensic Anthropology Lab. Smith was department chair until 1972.

FSU–Panama City

Florida State University at Panama City had its beginning in the early 70s. Recognizing the need for four-year degree programs, the Bay County community united in lobbying for an institution of higher learning. Shortly after, the Florida Board of Regents (BOR) instituted a plan to bring higher education to major population areas not within reasonable commuting distance of a state university. In 1972, the BOR directed the University of West Florida to establish a center in Panama City. Classes began with an enrollment of sixty-five elementary education students and a staff of two, using facilities of the Bay County School Board and Gulf Coast Community College (GCCC).

In 1976, the Bay County Commission purchased 17.5 acres between GCCC and the beautiful waters of North Bay, deeding the land to the state for the center. In 1981 the commission donated an additional 2.54 acres and three quadriplex apartments.

In the fall of 1982, the Florida Legislature and the BOR transferred administrative responsibility for the Panama City Center to Florida State. Groundbreaking began June 23, 1983, for the $9.1 million phase I development of FSU–Panama City. The new facilities were formally dedicated on March 22, 1986, with the administrative building named in honor of Senator Dempsey J. Barron, class of 1956, who sponsored the bill funding a permanent FSU facility.

Since the opening of the new campus in January 1987, FSU–Panama City has grown to almost 1,000 students supported by 12 bachelor's and 19 graduate degree programs. An additional 5.62-acre donation along the bay brings the campus to 25.66 acres. Building continues, following a master plan for development over the next decade. Fall 2000 marked the debut of full-time daytime programs, and new resident faculty have been hired. FSU–Panama City is pledged to academic excellence for area students.

Bonnie Williams, Executive Director of the Florida Commission on Ethics

In 1974 I had completed my coursework and exams toward my doctorate in English at FSU and was searching for a part-time or temporary job to keep body and soul (and those of my young son) together while writing my dissertation.

Through a friend who worked in Governor Askew's office, I learned that a new state commission on governmental ethics had been created and was being staffed. I applied and was interviewed in a public meeting by the full nine-member commission. Coincidentally, the first chairman, and the man who hired me, was Sandy D'Alemberte.

In 1987, I became executive director of the commission. I love my job but never finished my dissertation. I'll wager, however, that I'm one of the best-read public employees in Florida outside the university system.

Judy Pate (class of 1970): Florida State University Alumni Band

Over four 99¢ bottles of André's Cold Duck, four alums of FSU and the Marching Chiefs decided that what FSU needed was an Alumni Band! It was still a good idea after we sobered up. Soon, Curtis Falany, JoEllen Hicks (soon to be Mrs. Falany), and my husband Mike and I started to put things in motion. Sara Carter's help was enlisted and off we went.

Our first performance was homecoming of 1970. We raided the uniform room of "our" old uniforms and gave everyone a coat with the gold lamé overlay. The local beer distributor gave us styrofoam "straw" hats, and we put "FSU Alumni Band" hat bands around them.

We were only able to round up twenty-seven former Marching Chiefs, so to perform in the half-time show with the Chiefs we formed the feather at the top of the tomahawk. Of course we sat in the stands with the regular band members and showed them how good we still were at playing our instruments!

Over the next few years the Alumni Band really started to take off. We were thrilled the first time we had a man who was fifty years old participate in one homecoming. We couldn't believe that people that old could still play and march at the same time!

Since our humble beginnings we continue to march, 300 to 400 alums strong, at homecoming each year. We perform before the game as well as at half-time. Our sound is pretty good, no doubt owing to the fact that quite a few of us are band directors and professional musicians. I have no comment on the marching.

The Alumni Band now has an endowment fund made up entirely of donations from alums. From this, numerous scholarships are offered to students that participate in one of the School of Music bands.

We fifty-somethings and older are still having fun trying to march and play at the same time. And we still know the shouts familiar to all Marching Chiefs, "We've never lost a half-time show!" and "Marching Chiefs All the Damn Time!"

2001 marked the thirty-second performance of the Alumni Band.

The Alumni Band's first year,
homecoming 1977,
J. Michael Pate, drum major

Robert W. Fichter, Professor, Studio Art

My grandparents were pioneers in southwest Florida before the turn of the last century. And I remember swimming in Sarasota Bay in the 1950s when it was so clear that I remember the sea creatures as animated beings. . . .

In 1972, when I came to teach at FSU, it was as a returning prodigal son. Coming back from Los Angeles, the city of the future, I loved the fact that when I drove to Carrabelle to eat fresh seafood, a large real estate broker's sign loomed off to the left and proudly proclaimed: "Selling Florida's last frontier." It always struck me as if it were an ironic landscape detail from a T. S. Eliot poem.

My mother had taken a degree in home economics at FSU in 1929. She would rather have taken a degree in English literature, but she could read the writing on the wall. In a depression everyone still has to eat, and home economics got funded when English literature didn't.

So when Evon Streetman, who started the photography program at FSU, tried to lure me to teach in the Department of Art in the early 1970s, it was already a place of legend for me. The fact that the department had totally restructured itself on a new paradigm of art education seemed right to me. The traditional, compartmentalized, hierarchical areas of academic studio study (painting, printmaking, sculpture, photography, etc.) had been replaced by the workshop system in which each instructor was recognized as an artist first and a media specialist second. All media were equal in this system, and the students chose their instructors by the aesthetic and intellectual ideas presented by the instructors. Today the art program at FSU is one of the few schools in America that continues this approach to interdisciplinary study.

So I came back to Tallahassee to give something back, having received so much from people I met along the way: my childhood friends, teachers, family, and friends. This land of microclimes—of Spanish moss, resurrection fern, pines, oaks, cypress, the snapping turtle, and the pileated woodpecker—called me back.

Evon Streetman started the photography program at FSU.

Hand of Man, Robert Fichter, 1984 (cibachrome)

Joe McFadden (class of 1972): Ashmore's Store

Around 1970 while a student at FSU, I started to spend time at a Tallahassee institution, Ashmore's Antiques in Frenchtown. After a while, my friend Jim Parlapiano (also an FSU student) and I started a business buying and selling pecans in the shack adjacent to the store. Rob Ashmore let us have the shack rent-free because he liked having us, and the activity it generated, around.

Frenchtown was a vibrant community and Ashmore's seemed to me its epicenter. The place had a definite carnival atmosphere that drew many other students to buy used furniture and just to hang around. I remember thinking that I was in a place that had existed for me so far only in books.

These days whenever Ashmore introduces us to someone, he likes to say that we are his hippies and that he raised us, adding that when he met us we were against everything, even war!

His sense of humor is probably what attracted me most. He salutes fire trucks when they pass by, stands at attention and yells "Mail call!" when the mail is delivered, and marches out of his door every morning to put up the American flag.

To this day, when I am at an opening of my work, I can hear him saying to me, "You've got to talk to them, Pierre." He started calling me Pierre because he didn't think Joe was a suitable name for an artist. He has a wealth of practical advice.

I've painted Rob dozens of times and always find myself smiling as the face starts to take shape. He married my wife and me. When I asked him what "I pledge thee my troth" meant, he laughed and said, "Pierre, it's Latin."

Allys Palladino-Craig, Director, FSU Museum of Fine Arts

In the beginning was the Fine Arts Gallery—and the Gallery was good. There were some wild curators in the early years—one show was a conceptual piece consisting of massive gold frames with nothing behind them, just the empty wall. The carpet was electric blue (color-field painters hated that), and the walls were brick or raw concrete, which became intricately studded with screw-anchors. Every time a painting or photograph was hung for a new show, it was always at a different height from work hung in the last show. One enterprising graduating artist, Marsha Orr, put a bean in each empty anchor in her section of the gallery, watering them for the week preceding the opening. By opening night, of course, they had all sprouted.

Over the seasons of exhibitions beginning in 1970, and through the procession (er, succession) of directors—Bruce Dempsey, Len Kleckner, Marsha Orr (interim), Albert Stewart, and myself—the walls were eventually faced in with neutral board and the carpet changed to a sober gray. We have worked hard to make the space more art friendly and we have come of age as an institution, now named the Museum of Fine Arts. The changes reflect not only the permanent collection holdings (roughly 4000 works of art), but also the new stature of the museum, its place in the Museum Studies Program at the university, and the increasingly ambitious and nationally competitive curatorial and publication projects undertaken here. We continue to divide our calendar between exhibitions which are awarded prestigious grants and write art history, and the lively graduating artist and faculty exhibitions (which occasionally write local history—more letters to the editor than were thought possible). The Museum of Fine Arts is a vital and colorful mix, a place where scholarship and creative one-upmanship balance in the limelight of public scrutiny. There is never a dull moment, the programs are an effervescent spectrum of media and points of view, and the museum is a lovely place to visit—either by yourself or with a K–12 cast of thousands. Welcome.

Top: *The Merchant*, a painting of Rob Ashmore by Joe McFadden

Theatre dean Gil Lazier and actress Faye Dunaway, an FSU alum, in the mid-1980s

"When I began working at FSU, there was no such thing as a word processor. Calculations were made with thirteen-column pads, pencils, and electronic calculators. Joe Hiett came up with the idea for the perfect beverage at the reception for Claude Pepper's honorary doctorate. Dr. Pepper, of course."

JOHN KALB

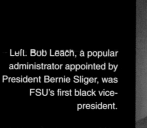

Left: Bob Leach, a popular administrator appointed by President Bernie Sliger, was FSU's first black vice-president.

Right: Dobie Flowers, FSU's first African-American homecoming queen, 1970

Bernie Sliger, who doesn't drive, was famous during his presidency for his walks across campus. The author of this profile, Linda Harkey, is an FSU alum.

On a Friday morning in early June, President Bernard F. Sliger walks out the front door of the colonial revival house, built in 1981, which serves as the official Florida State University residence. When he moved into the 6,890-square-foot house seven years ago, Sliger said it was much too grand to be a home. From the hill on which the house is situated, Sliger can look through the magnolia trees and across Tennessee Street to the brick-and-concrete, rectangular Nuclear Research Building, which houses the tandem Van de Graaff accelerator. He will walk across campus, past at least a dozen more buildings, before he reaches his office in Westcott, a four-story brick structure dating from 1910.

Buildings on campus range in style from Dodd Hall, built of brick in 1923 with an archway and an ornate doorway inscribed "The half of knowledge is to know where to find knowledge," to the Physics Department's Keen Building, constructed in 1963, which bears no inscription and has no archway and is a rectilinear monument to wordless induction and intuition.

For the past month, a knee injury has kept the president from making his almost daily walks through campus. He carries a walking cane. He wears a short-sleeved dacron and linen guayabera, gray trousers, and Italian loafers of very fine leather. In his shirt pocket are two rosebuds that he noticed as he was crossing the grounds of the house. Throughout the year, the desks of his staff members are brightened by camellias, roses, and gardenias, that Sliger notices as he walks to work.

Two men who are resurfacing a driveway say hello; a student jogging across campus calls and waves. A faculty member walking to the library smiles and says, "Oh, hi, Bernie."

Sliger walks by the business school annex under construction. It is of a livelier style than the surrounding buildings, but its red brick and scale make it look at home.

Noticing that one of the rose buds has fallen out of his pocket, Sliger looks back along the chain link fence that surrounds the construction area. "Someone probably picked it up," he says. Over little things that go wrong, he doesn't fuss. When it comes to big projects, however, he is tenacious until they are realities.

When he became president, Sliger envisioned his priorities in the form of four buildings that would house major programs. The Center for Professional Development, which coordinates continuing education courses and noncredit courses and symposia, moved into its new conference center in 1982. The annex to the business building was another. The School of Engineering, a joint project of Florida State and Florida A&M, was to be built in Innovation Park. Last came the Science Library, supporting a group of science programs that Sliger thinks are the best in the State University System. . . .

Linda Harkey, *Florida State*, 1983

In 1978 President Jimmy Carter's mother, Lillian Gordy Carter, seen here with President Bernie Sliger, received an honorary degree for her work in public service.

Greta Lee Sliger (Ph.D. 1997)

While my dad was president of FSU, it was memorable having an opportunity to live in the president's house. It seems strange that it's no longer a residence because it really was a great house (and probably convenient for my dad since he didn't drive). We had a lot of social functions in the backyard, which included some great bands, several celebrities, and good parties. At that time The Pub was right down the road and Pugs gas station and oyster bar were next door.

I remember one dramatic cold snap. Some students in a dorm that had lost heat came to our house, asking if they could have shelter (most likely assuming we were nice and toasty). My mom said, "of course," and gave them all blankets since our house had lost all power too. During that same time, one student called and asked my dad if he could do something about the weather.

I also remember the football games at FSU from the time we moved to town in 1972, when you could always get in free at half-time and tickets were just a few bucks, to the later years when FSU was always ranked in the top three teams. At that time the press box was about the size of a small kitchen, and the only refreshments were peanuts and popcorn. You had to make sure you got there early to get a seat.

Probably the best memory for me at FSU was FINALLY graduating with my Ph.D. and having my dad (who was retired from the presidency then) hood me during the ceremony. That made all of the work worthwhile.

The door slammed shut on the van, an old van at that. Inside were twelve young athletes crunched together, one of them actually wedged into the space where the door closes (before seat belts were required). The destination was somewhere in North Carolina for an intercollegiate athletic match. They left in the early morning, planning to play that evening and then crunch back into the van for the return. There was no money for motel rooms and barely enough for gas and food (fast food, of course). The year was 1977. The team was the Lady Seminole volleyball team.

This was not a unique situation for any of the women's intercollegiate teams. It was the norm at that time. What kept gnawing at me, almost making me sick, was that all of the men's teams were either flying or riding a comfortable bus to their matches. They were staying overnight when necessary and eating at sit-down restaurants. I kept asking myself, "Why would anyone treat a daughter so differently from a son?" The question came to me even though I had no children. Now that I am a parent, it absolutely flabbergasts me that such disparate treatment of our daughters was so acceptable. I made a pledge to myself that day (having been in the job a total of two weeks). This would not happen again—even if we had to decrease the number of games until we could get the necessary funds. This was unfair and unsafe!

Interestingly, I don't believe the men involved (mostly men, but not all) were conscious of unfairness. Or, they may have been able to close an eye, hiding behind the outdated notion that competition and sports were not good or proper for women. Still, being so committed to the growth of men's sports, mainly football and basketball, some probably saw the development of women's sports as a threat (just as some fear the growth of nonrevenue Olympic sports for men). I really never felt that the women's program should cause the demise of the men's program: *That wasn't a win for anyone!*

FSU athletic director John Bridgers, a progressive and fair-minded leader, was very supportive of innovative solutions and helped to shape my philosophy. I believed then, and still do today, that we had to find new money—from Seminole Boosters, concessions, or even state appropriations—to get the women's programs started.

Lo and behold, it worked. The budget swelled from $163,000 with no full-time coaches, no facilities, and no uniforms or equipment to $1.5 million with full-time coaches, scholarships, travel dollars, etc. By 1980, the FSU women's program became a dominant force in intercollegiate athletics. Within two years, we won five national championships: two in softball with coach Jo Ann Graf, one in golf with coach Verlyn Giles, one in outdoor track, and one in indoor track with coach Roger Smith.

Equally exciting, however, was that FSU's success extended to all of Florida's universities. In 1979 we lobbied the Florida Legislature, and with the leadership of Representative Herb Morgan and Senator Dempsey Barron, we did something no other state had ever done (or has since). The Legislature approved an appropriation to provide equity in sports statewide, enabling thousands of young women to become the best athletes they could be.

At the same time, Andy Miller, executive director of the Boosters, had the wisdom and vision to hire a full-time fundraiser for women's athletics. Debbie Mason Derzypolski took on the challenge gleefully. Needless to say, with an enormous task and some political resistance, she had to work incredibly hard. But she not only raised hundreds of thousands of dollars, she helped change people's attitudes and feelings about women's sports. The rest is history and statistics.

FSU pitcher Christy Larson, 3rd team All-American, 1991

T.K. Wetherell (class of 1967, M.S. 1968, Ph.D. 1974): University Center

FSU's $96 million University Center, which wraps around Doak Campbell Stadium, was built in 1993. It is named for T.K. Wetherell.

The credit for University Center really goes to Mode Stone and Coyle Moore, who started talking about the idea back in 1963. I was a nineteen-year-old freshman football player at the time, and Dr. Stone took a liking to me. He was the dean of education, and he really liked football.

Dr. Stone founded the Southern Scholarship Foundation and had known my dad, Thomas J. Wetherell, who, as a vice-president of Sears, had a part in making donations to the foundation. Coyle Moore, for whom FSU's athletics complex is named, was dean of social work. Together, Moore and Stone had a vision for FSU.

Dr. Stone came out to practice one day, and when we were walking off the field, he said that one day FSU would be like Notre Dame and Oklahoma in football—a real national power. And he said that the stadium, instead of being used just five Saturdays a year for football games and occasionally for ROTC drills, would be full of buildings. He said there would be classrooms and dormitories—an entire education facility.

Fast forward to 1988. I'm speaker designate and appropriations chairman in the Florida House. Bernie Sliger, who was president then, and Andy Miller, who was head of the Seminole Boosters, came up with what they called a "crazy idea" they wanted to discuss.

We went to Anthony's Restaurant for dinner that night, and right there on the tablecloth we designed a concept for what would become the University Center. It had everything, including classrooms and offices, but also condos with hot tubs and a parking garage. We even made plans for a Marriott Hotel. We made such a mess of the tablecloth we told Anthony we'd buy it, and we did.

Chancellor Charlie Reed shot down the condos, hot tubs, and hotel. He didn't want private involvement. But we took the plan to FSU's facilities planners, who put together a real proposal.

That year Bob Martinez was governor and Pete Dunbar was his chief of staff. Pete was a strong FSU Booster, and the Boosters agreed to raise $10 million. We took it to the Legislature and found money to pay for it in a lot of places: education, transportation, community affairs, and the gross receipts tax. That's really how it happened. And to me the only thing that's missing is the parking garage. And maybe those hot tubs.

student affairs Lu Goldhagen, he met personally with the parents and relatives of the victims.

On Monday, 1,400 students and faculty members filed quietly into Ruby Diamond Auditorium for memorial services for Margaret Bowman and Lisa Levy, and to pray for the recovery of Karen Chandler, Kathy Kleiner, and Cheryl Thomas. The sense of sadness was so profound and overwhelming it affected even those who had come to report. One young reporter from the *Tallahassee Democrat* admitted feeling like an intruder as he conducted interviews afterward. "I wondered: Is it worth bothering these people just so someone can read one good quote in the morning paper?," reporter James Cramer said later of his assignment. "I took one look at the tears on a young woman's face, shut my notebook, and left campus."

In spite of the grief and terror, no panic swept Florida State. Lu Goldhagen recalled that the students "reacted beautifully. They were calm and did what was needed for their safety." For months afterward the university improved its security measures, including the escort service and the security guards for residences.

For the survivors of the attack, however, recovery was an act of courage repeated daily. Cheryl Thomas recuperated in Virginia. A dance major, she worked out daily at a local studio, afraid that the damage to her inner ear would permanently affect her dancing. Karen Chandler returned to classes in March, hopeful that people would respond to her normally and reserve their sympathy for the parents of Margaret Bowman and Lisa Levy. Kathy Kleiner remained in seclusion.

At some point after Ted Bundy was in jail for murder, Dr. Sliger received a call from Harry Morrison, the state's attorney in Tallahassee: "Morrison asked me to go to a telephone where I could talk in private, which I did. Harry said that Ted Bundy was going to admit to killing the Chi Omega sorority sisters and would then be given a life sentence, if I agreed. I thought about it for a minute and told him that it was all right. I thought it would be good to have his admission of guilt and be put away for life. However, he had escaped a time or two from previous prisons, and that was worrying."

Later, Bundy decided not to make a confession. He was then brought before a jury in South Florida, where he was convicted of the murders and sentenced to death. By that time, Sliger said that he "was pleased that Bundy hadn't confessed earlier." Ted Bundy was executed.

Florida State

"I thought, how can I help them?"

PRESIDENT BERNARD SLIGER

"I had several offers when I retired from Cambridge in 1969. Princeton, Stony Brook in New York. Others. Some of the offers were very nice, very comfortable. But I chose to come to Florida State because it is a center of excellence."

NOBEL LAUREATE PAUL ADRIAN MAURICE DIRAC

The universe according to Paul Adrian Maurice Dirac is an awesome scape, somewhere over the rainbow of common sense, where "God's language" is spoken and parallel lines meet. Faster is slower in Dirac's world. Up may be down, pushing may be pulling, and things rarely are what they seem to be.

Dirac, called the "mystic of the atom" during his Cambridge days, is Florida State University's most impressive monument to scientific genius. "What projects am I working on?" he replies to a question. "I am mulling it all over."

Dirac dreams of finding one set of laws to explain the whole universe and its workings. No map can describe such a riddling place "without introducing irrelevancies," Dirac says. To draw its picture is "like a blind man sensing a snowflake. One touch and it's gone."

Matter is nothing but jiggling waves. Sometimes energy hurtles about like legions of tiny bowling balls; sometimes it scatters like ripples on a pond. Dirac's equation, which earned him the Nobel Prize, treats it as both at once. His is the world of modern theoretical physics, the world of quantum mechanics, relativity, black holes. The Big Bang, *Star Wars*, *E.T.* and Dr. Who were born there. Space flight, electronic communications, computer technology, and automatic garage-door openers were hatched there. And the secrets of where we came from, what we are, and where we're going are hiding there.

"God used beautiful mathematics in creating the world," Dirac says. "Beautiful but not simple. My theories are based on a faith that there is reason for all the numbers nature provides us with. You will learn more out of this than from studying the Bible."

Dirac's research facilities consist of the following: a pencil, several sheets of blank paper, a thumb-sized rubber eraser, and the sharp, clear prism of his mind. He accepts no voluntary degrees, hates politics and never votes, explains little ("Books have been written on that," he says, rather sharply), rarely gives interviews or answers letters, and is often a mystery even to those in his field.

But there is another side, too. In Tallahassee, he is known to many as a fascinating lecturer, witty story teller, delightful host, and charming companion. He reads Agatha Christie, Ellery Queen, and Sherlock Holmes; watches *Nova*, *Masterpiece Theatre*, and mystery shows; loves classical music and thinks Tallahassee drivers are a perfect fright. "Away from his work," says FSU music professor Edward Kilenyi, a family friend, "Paul is like everybody else. He just doesn't chitchat very much."

"I had several offers when I retired from Cambridge in 1969," Dirac said. "Princeton, Stony Brook in New York. Others. Some of the offers were very nice, very comfortable. But I chose to come to Florida State because it is a center of excellence."

"He likes it here because we treat him just like one of the boys," adds physics professor Joe Lannutti. "And because we're the top physics department in the Southeast. Dirac himself compared our program to that at Cambridge. He came because the research is here. Not because of the sunshine."

Midway through his eightieth year, Dirac is stoop-shouldered and frail. His rumpled black suit is almost a metaphor for Einstein's concept of infinity: Its 1950s style has gone full circle and may soon be back. "He is one of the two worst dressed men I have ever seen," concedes Margit Dirac, his wife of forty-six years. "Einstein was the other. But then at Cambridge it was bad form to dress; they all looked like tramps."

In 1933 Dirac shared the Nobel Prize with Erwin Schroedinger, the physicist whose quantum-wave theory he completed. Although his equation explained fully the mechanics of the atom, it set Dirac on a fifty-year quest that continues today. "Dirac will not be satisfied until it is possible to describe all physics as one kind of universe," says assistant Dr. Leopold Halpern, who has his own theory of how the search will end. "A physicist only stops physics when he doesn't breathe any more. And then for his tombstone, I suspect Dirac will say, 'Put nothing on it. Others must find the way.'"

Andy Lindstrom, *Research in Review*, June 1983
The FSU Dirac Science Library is named for the Nobel Prize winner, who died in 1984.

Opposite: Nobel Laureate Paul Dirac joined the Physics Department faculty in 1970.

Former Florida Supreme Court Justice B.K. Roberts speaks at the dedication of the College of Law administration building named in his honor, 1971.

"Florida State has held a special place in my mind because my two aunts and my mother had attended it as FSCW and later FSU. Coming from the small Florida panhandle town of Valparaiso, FSU struck me as a self-contained city in and of itself."

NATHANIEL BOWIE RANSOM (CLASS OF 1984)

"*Jim Macmillan was the epitome of the liberally educated scholar and creative thinker. He loved his family, he cared about his students, he cared about his colleagues, he cared deeply about Florida State University, and he gave of himself to make it as good as it could be.*"

STEVE EDWARDS, DEAN OF THE FACULTIES

Kathy Spetz (class of 1971): Critter Creations

American sports fans may not know Kathy Spetz, but many know her creations. If you've ever seen the Pittsburgh Pirates' "Pirate Parrot," or the bull mascot of the Birmingham Bulls Hockey Team, or the University of Georgia's red and black bulldog, then you've seen Spetz's work.

Top: James Macmillan (1935–1998), Professor of Education, served FSU for twenty-eight years.

Right: Dean of Faculties Steve Edwards inducted into Mortar Board in 1993. From L, Edwards, Vonda Lynch and Carol Darling, Professor of Family and Child Sciences

In September 1980, in Paris, I picked up a copy of the *International Herald-Tribune*. Every American in Europe reads the *Trib* to keep up with news from home. In one issue what caught my eye immediately was a picture of Burt Reynolds and a headline: "Burt Reynolds makes large gift to Florida State University."

James P. Jones, *Florida State*, 1981

Above: Players hoist Metro Conference trophy after the basketball tournament, March 9, 1991. L to R: Douglas Edwards, Michael Polite, Lorenzo Hands, and Rodney Dobard.

Opposite: Head trainer Don (Doc) Fauls, Burt Reynolds on the field before the Western Carolina game, November 16, 1985 when the Boosters presented Fauls with a station wagon for his years of service.

Selena Fleskes (Ransom) (class of 1983)

My fondest memories of Florida State are the home football games. I was able to attend all of the home games except for one. On that particular Saturday I needed to study for an upcoming exam, so I grudgingly stayed home. What a mistake! I lived in an apartment near Doak Campbell Stadium and could not concentrate on my studies because of the cheers echoing from the stadium. Although I do not remember how I did on that particular exam, I never missed a home game again.

"Tom-toms starting early in the day of the Florida game and playing up to game time; Sammy Seminole doing back flips; meeting and marrying my wife while at FSU."

TOM H. BURR (CLASS OF 1972)

In the afterglow of last night's win against Brigham Young, Florida State football fans will be easy enough to spot today: sleepy eyes but cockeyed grins, and shoulders thrown back a centimeter or two.

It covers Tallahassee like the kudzu and could last for several days—this unremitting sense of satisfaction that a winning team inspires. Particularly this team already judged best in the nation.

Football remains the most cathartic spectator sport. Talk with fans around North Florida this week and you'll understand: football is late summer's elixir. "A winning team stimulates a lot of interest from the backwoods," said retiree Jack Richey, drinking coffee at Governor's Square. "They may have never gone to college—not FSU or anywhere else—but when the home team starts winning, it's Our Team."

Success is a patina that can permanently change the character of a place, and its luster reflects well. FSU is nationally known because of football, not because of the magnet lab, noted John Calvin, a faithful 1948 graduate. And yet FSU did get that magnet lab.

Business owners notice the way a winning football team translates into cash. In gas stations, T-shirt shops, newsstands, restaurants, it's a fact—people spend more when they're in the feel-good mood a winning team provokes.

Through football, fans see the world a little differently and find out things about themselves. Down on the field, the game may turn teen-age boys into grown men. But in the stands, it allows grown men to be little boys. It lets them play at war safely, legally and without the moral weight.

"I'm so excited I can hardly stand it," confessed Scott Dailey on the eve of last night's game. "No question there's this macho-marine mentality—the endurance of pain, the self-for the-team idea. It goes back to the gladiators. No matter how intellectual or sophisticated we are, there's something primeval about football. God help us."

The attraction is there for women, too. "It's kind of like those women who love Harleys," guessed Marsha Orr, an art dealer and a confessed Seminole maniac. "Women often respond to real overt power things that maybe they didn't always have access to, being brought up ladies."

She also sees it as performance art. Think of it, if you can, as an event passing through time. Form dissolves into chaos. It's the universal struggle.

When the Seminoles are winning, the galvanizing effect on a community can be healthy. People as different as night and day find common ground on the issue of their football team, and people invariably relish the things that bind us together. "But how weird," added Orr, "to have 60,000 people gathered in a mass of architectural scaffolding, and they've all got their attention focused on a single thing."

Exploitation of the players bothers the best of fans, who wish the players were more prepared for life after football—particularly when there's a good chance their bodies may be permanently broken. This detraction from the sport is hard to ignore when, from the first game to the last bowl, we see painful variations of tackles like the one that leveled Amp Lee.

Thoughtful fans often admit to feelings of ambiguity about football, even as they admit to its seduction. Professional culture-basher Hunter Thompson once confessed: "All I've ever claimed to be is a nice guy and an athlete."

One feminist said she likes the way football allows men to touch each other unashamedly. "They whack each other on the back; they tenderly comfort each other," she said.

An ex-high-school athlete who understands the exploitation and brutality nevertheless confided: "If I could sell my soul like the fellow did in *Damn Yankees*, I'd be 6-foot-2 and a professional quarterback with a quick drop and a quick release. That or a flamenco dancer."

Mary Ann Lindley, *Tallahassee Democrat*, August 30, 1991 (reprinted in *Saint Bobby and the Barbarians*, by Ben Brown, Doubleday, 1992)

Opposite: Charlie Ward with the Heisman Trophy at a celebration in Doak Campbell Stadium, December 15, 1993.

"Whenever I hear the Marching Chiefs hit the fight song or play the alma mater,
I still get goosebumps. From orientation through graduation, I never once
regretted my decision to attend FSU. I even went on to marry an FSU alum!"

JAY WELLS (CLASS OF 1991)

"I remember thinking Bobby Bowden was an untouchable, larger-than-life icon at
FSU. While I was a student, I was walking in the Moore Athletic Center and noticed
Bobby Bowden walking toward me. When he said 'hello,' I looked back to see who was
behind me but found no one. I was shocked. He was saying hello to me."

It is September 20, 1960, in Tallahassee, Florida, and as you twirl the selector knob on your television you notice the sounds of a new channel coming to life. You're greeted by a professor in tweed who welcomes you to English 101. This is the start of "Educational Television" in Tallahassee, the baby born to grow into the multifaceted source of engrossing and enlightening entertainment that we now call Public Television.

At that time, housed in Dodd Hall, the cameras rolled with a budget of $100,000, shared with WFSU-FM, and a staff of twelve. By 1978 the budget for WFSU-TV alone was $1.2 million, covering fifty-three full-time and ten part-time employees. Ed Herp was the general manager and Jim Moran was program director.

Shows like *Sesame Street*, *Nova*, and *Masterpiece Theatre* changed the look of WFSU-TV and all the member stations.

In 1979 about 10% of Channel 11's overall schedule was devoted to local programming, including *Prime Time*, a news show, and *Vibrations*, a program illuminating the black perspective on community affairs. Producer-director Heinz Backfish helped produce *Dance at Dawn*, a blend of music, movement, and nature that was the first WFSU-TV production shown nationally by PBS.

Patrick Keating, an FSU alum who directed *Prime Time* in 1979, was the program director for WFSU-TV from 1984 to 1987. During this period he produced the first live, statewide, call-in show featuring then-governor Bob Graham.

Keating left for other industry work but returned in March 2001 as general manager of WFSU-TV/FM, responsible for all operations of FSU's three radio stations, two television stations, one cable channel, and a statewide television service called the Florida Channel. What strikes him most is how much the station's mission has remained the same: "We still see as part of our mission to bring our listeners and viewers closer to their government and to vital issues. Another focus is children. We are a PBS 'Ready to Learn' station, with literacy at the top of our agenda.

Ira Shorr, *Florida State*, Winter 1997, with additional information from Patrick Keating, 2001

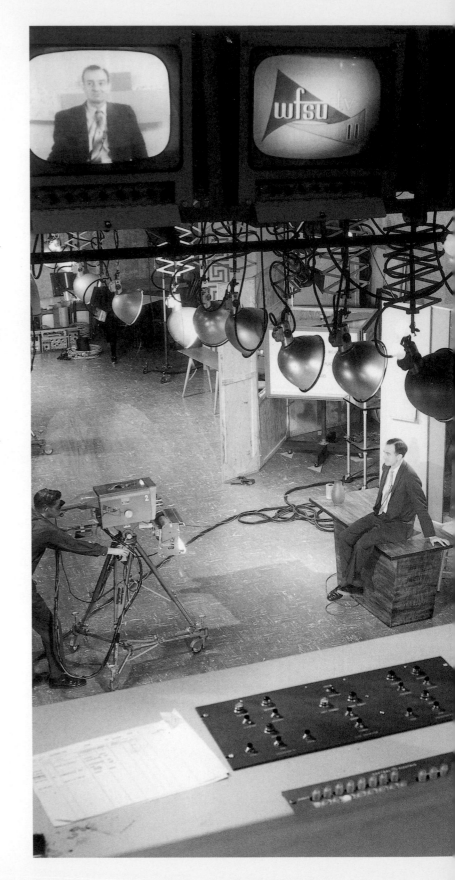

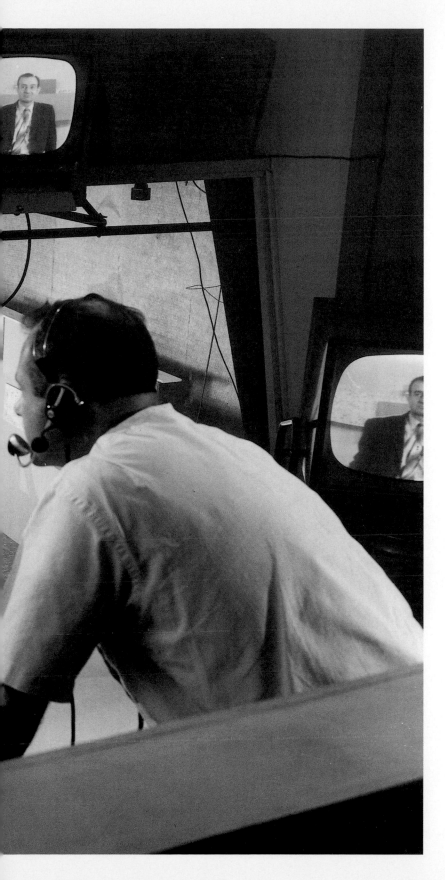

Left: A set within WFSU-TV's studios housed in Dodd Hall, 1971

Right: Stephen Winters (retired 1989), a popular dean and professor of geology, won the Ross Oglesby award in 1973. The award, given by the Gold Key Honor Society, is for distinguished service to the university.

Kim MacQueen (class of 1988)

When I first showed up to write $10 student government features for the *Flambeau*, I sat just outside the newsroom with Steve, the advisor, in a little neutral-area office. I was afraid to go in the newsroom. People threw verbal barbs and a blue plastic bass at each other while they typed out stories on grimy Tandy 1000s. The south side of the newsroom was filled with lefties talking about politics I didn't understand; on the north side were sports and arts writers discussing games and music I'd never seen or heard; and everybody had some weird nickname.

The *Flambeau* would teach me about writing features for a newspaper, Steve said, but "nobody's getting rich in there." In fact most of the newsroom was stretching convenience store sodas to make them last all day and making big meals of crackers filched from Wendy's. I learned how to write and edit news and features, how to form an opinion and lay out a newspaper, why REM sold out, what apartheid was, and why it's probably not a good idea to form romantic relationships with coworkers. At my bridal shower before I married a staffer, I got a haphazardly wrapped, fish-shaped present; it was the blue plastic bass.

I took the news of the *Flambeau*'s death the way I might if I heard about an old drinking buddy falling to some wasting disease. It was a scrappy little rag that got it right a lot of the time and wasn't afraid to say what it thought, damn the consequences. There wasn't anything else like it around then, and there isn't now.

Raymond E. Fielding

Before there was a film school at Florida State University, a film "institute" was proposed and created as a first step. Later, a number of people within FSU, as well as external consultants, contributed to the creation of a complete School of Motion Picture, Television and Recording Arts. Within FSU, Provost Gus Turnbull, his assistant Dr. Russ Kropp, and Dr. Ted Clevenger, dean of the College of Communications, were especially active in the founding of a major film school with appropriate facilities and both graduate and undergraduate programs. I was proud to become the school's founding dean in 1990.

Although the film institute never functioned actively, it still exists as a potential vehicle for future expansion of the film program. In the 1980s one person who contributed to the original institute idea was Richard Portman, an Academy Award–winning sound director from the Hollywood film industry. In 1995, he was recruited to the film school faculty and has continued as one of the school's most active full-time instructors.

I grew up in Hollywood, California, during the golden age of the Hollywood studio system. It was a system that operated like a family and produced excellence technically and artistically. All of the facilities, equipment, and personnel needed to make a movie were organized together on one lot, or under one roof.

I began to dream of one day, somewhere, taking the best aspects of the old studio system and recreating it to teach a young cadre of filmmakers. I had almost given up on my dream when, in late 1983, I made my first trip to Tallahassee and Florida State University.

After my first trip to Florida State I knew that this was where my dream belonged. The possibility of establishing a virtual "teaching studio" seemed possible. FSU had excellent, established schools and departments of theatre, communication, music, creative writing, visual arts, law and engineering: all the elements needed to make movies. The state of Florida was interested in developing a film industry, and young students and filmmakers were eager for education and opportunities.

After traveling a long and winding road, with the usual ups and downs, this collective idea/dream not only evolved into a film school, but into a virtual studio, encompassing both undergraduate and graduate programs. The Florida State University School of Motion Picture, Television, and Recording Arts would be housed in an excellent facility, with ample equipment and a bright future.

Augustus B. Turnbull III

FSU Provost Gus Turnbull's death in 1991 was a loss to the university and to many admiring friends and colleagues. This is an excerpt from Dr. Turnbull's remarks on being presented with the Westcott Distinguished Service Medal, November 13, 1991.

I cannot help but note the public service connection of the two previous Westcott medalists. There is no single person in whose footsteps I would be more honored to follow than Governor Leroy Collins—a statesman and friend. Representative Herb Morgan demonstrated in the greatest measure how to effectively support higher education in demanding budget times.

I share with the former recipients a keen sense of the importance of public service. I have endeavored to recognize the valued role a university can and must play in public service. We, in academe, must maintain our intellectual integrity—we must never dilute our standards—but we must also remember we are part and parcel of the state and nation in which we teach and garner knowledge, and we must respect our obligation to share the richness of our learning. Public service is an equal part of the triad of functions of a university—teaching, research, and public service.

Thomas Jefferson, one of our most learned presidents, founded the University of Virginia after leaving the presidency. As a graduate of "Mr. Jefferson's university," I often turn to him for wisdom in addressing the academic problems of the day. Jefferson met discouragement after discouragement in his efforts to form an "academical village." Furthermore, Jefferson's architectural plans for the university—now regarded as a work of beauty—and more recently emulated by our own Law School Green—were ridiculed as "too ornate and extravagant." When the Virginia General Assembly balked at approving $15,000 for the university, Jefferson replied: "It is vain to give us the name of a university without the means of making it so."

Our university is bigger then all of us. It is not just a collection of our minds and souls—but a preserve of the minds and souls of the students and faculty who have gone before us. Let us not be so arrogant as to think that any one individual, any one economic downturn, even any one discouraging football season—will diminish this great university and all that it stands for.

Four hundred years from now, Florida State University will still be here—fostered by those of you who were steadfast at all times. Bolstered by those of you who recognized that your legacy—whether as a student, faculty, administrator, or friend of the university—has meaning and purpose beyond the present day.

Gus Turnbull, 1988

Tom Randle

In the fall of 1980, I met with the professor in charge of internships for graduate students in the College of Social Sciences. He told me that no internships were available in Leon County for students working on a master's in public administration. I explained that I was living with, and taking care of, my elderly grandmother and could not leave town. He said, "Too bad. If you cannot move to central or south Florida, you'll have to delay graduation until you work something out." I left his office discouraged and angry.

Later that week I heard of an internship in the governor's Cabinet and Legislative Affairs Office. I got the position, but without credits from FSU. I met provost Gus Turnbull, and after explaining my problem, he made sure that I received the credit I needed for graduation and offered encouragement.

What I find wonderful about FSU are my memories of Gus Turnbull. He was one of the people who treated me like family and not just one of many students passing through.

Left: Norman Earl Thagard, an FSU alum in engineering (BA 1965, MA 1966) also earned a medical degree before qualifying for a spot as an astronaut on the space shuttle Challenger. He is a faculty member in the College of Engineering at FSU, where the Thagard Student Health Center is named for him. Thagard is married to an FSU alum, the former Rex Kirby Johnson.

Right: L to R: Chancellor Charlie Reed, Board of Regents; U.S. Vice-President Al Gore; Director Jack Crow, Mag Lab; Governor Lawton Chiles; and U.S. Senator Bob Graham at dedication of the National High Magnetic Field Laboratory, 1994

Opposite: National High Magnetic Field Laboratory

In many ways, my FSU career has been a vocational heaven. I have been fortunate to have challenging, creative work through which I indulge a passion for international travel. I began my current position in 1992 under Jon Dalton, the vice-president for student affairs. Jon had come to FSU in 1989 already committed to a staff exchange with his counterpart at the University of Costa Rica (UCR). He named the program SALSA (Student Affairs Linking Student Affairs).

The SALSA exchanges consisted of reciprocal visits of four to five student community leaders. During our visits, we witnessed students teaching music and computer skills in community centers and devising disaster plans for residents of *precarios* (squatter communities).

During a 1993 visit to Costa Rica, we met Professor Margarita Meseguer, an agricultural economist who suggested that SALSA bring eight to ten students to assist UCR students with a study concerning adolescents. FSU in turn would later host UCR students and involve them in similar community service.

From that seed, Beyond Borders: International Service and Cultural Exchanges grew. We added exchanges with the University of the West Indies in 1995 and with the Technical University in Dresden, Germany, in 1998. As of May 2001, roughly 200 FSU students and 20 staff have participated. The goals of the exchanges remain the same: to provide students with a low-cost, short-term international experience, to immerse students in the host university and community, to learn about community challenges through service, to foster friendships, and to deepen knowledge of the host country's language, culture, history, society.

National High Magnetic Field Laboratory

The National High Magnetic Field Laboratory (NHMFL) at Florida State University, known informally as the mag lab, is the only laboratory of its kind in the western hemisphere and one of only nine such facilities in the world. It is the world's largest and highest-powered magnet laboratory and has developed a series of world-record magnets for research in all areas of science and medicine.

In 1990 the National Science Foundation announced that the NHMFL was awarded in a peer-review competition, replacing the National Bitter Magnet Laboratory that had been at MIT for twenty-eight years. The National Science Foundation announced the new award on August 17, 1990, which is the birthday of the laboratory director, Dr. Jack Crow. A consortium among FSU, the Los Alamos National Laboratory, and the University of Florida, the mag lab attracts some 500 users annually from universities, private industry, and government worldwide.

Tuition increase protest march on capitol, 1991. L to R: President Dale Lick, Commissioner of Education Betty Castor, Board of Regents member Jim Smith

Dale W. Lick, President, 1991–1993

Capital Campaign

When I arrived on campus in the fall of 1991, a Capital Campaign, the first ever at Florida State University, had been much discussed. But the preparatory research had not yet been done or the final goal set. We went forward with these efforts in earnest, finding good support for a major campaign. We did research, put the major committees and chairs in place, and compiled the "want" lists from alumni, students, faculty, staff, and administrators for a case statement. My personal visiting of key donors and participants went well. However, when our consultants came in with a recommended five-year campaign goal, it was only $140 million. I challenged them with $200 million as a minimum goal, citing the popularity of FSU, its quality and growing momentum for even greater stature, and especially the deep spirits of its alumni and friends.

They countered that a goal of $200 million was folly and didn't have a chance of success.

Believing the consulting team had missed key fundraising factors, I convinced the FSU Foundation board to set the goal at $200 million, which scared some board members while inspiring others. Our campaign efforts even before the official campaign announcement brought in well over $100 million. As the campaign momentum grew in leaders, advocates, and donors, the goal was met early and increased. Our first-ever Capital Campaign netted, ultimately, over $300 million.

A Magnetic Nobel Laureate

One of the university's most important advancements was attracting Nobel Laureate John Robert Schrieffer to the faculty as an Eminent Professor and chief scientist of the National High Magnetic Field Laboratory.

FSU and its partners had just won the National Science Foundation contract for the laboratory away from the Massachusetts Institute of Technology. Now FSU had to deliver on its big promises for the lab. Could FSU actually land one of the giants in the field? With determination and great support from the chancellor of the Board of Regents, we did.

Dr. Schrieffer, with two colleagues, won the Nobel Prize for physics in 1972. He published the first successful theory to explain superconductivity: motion unhindered by friction. Now he was Chancellor's Professor at the University of California/Santa Barbara. After Professor Schrieffer visited our campus and interviewed everyone in sight, he said that he wanted to meet the president-elect before making a final decision. That put me center stage. On one of my visits to Tallahassee before assuming the presidency, I was leaving just as Professor Schrieffer was arriving. So, we met at the Tallahassee airport for our official visit. He was filled with exciting questions and visions, and I knew he really was precisely the person for our lead scholar position. Apparently our meeting went well. Dr. Schrieffer almost immediately agreed to join the university and laboratory teams.

Professor Schrieffer's coming gave FSU science a quantum boost in reputation, expectation, and quality. His presence prepared the way for many other preeminent scholars to join our efforts. The National High Magnetic Field Laboratory is now the premier facility of its kind in the world, and Florida State University's reputation and scholarly stature have been enhanced immeasurably as a result.

Nobel Prize physicist J. Robert Schrieffer of the National High Magnetic Field Laboratory at FSU was the first faculty appointment to the Magnet Lab.

Diversity

During the 1980s, colleges across the United States made unusual progress in the area of diversity, especially as it related to minorities and women, yet all the while battling major resistance. However, as the decade of the 90s began, FSU assertively built a foundation for even greater diversity. The most visible signs were two university-wide commissions, the Commission on Pluralism and the Commission on Women. Through the work of these commissions and the Office of Affirmative Action, along with many individuals' leadership and encouragement, new mindsets truly changed the campus culture. Diversity grew in virtually all areas of the university, and FSU became known as one of the State University System's most progressive leaders. As a result, Florida State University was changed forever and moved toward the twenty-first century with a commitment to the worth and dignity of all people.

PRESIDENT **TALBOT (SANDY) D'ALEMBERTE** (1994–PRESENT)

SESQUICENTENNIAL FSU

President Talbot (Sandy) D'Alemberte

Dr. Dale Lick resigned as president of FSU on August 31, 1993, and chose to remain at FSU as a full professor of mathematics. ¶ Talbot (Sandy) D'Alemberte was appointed president of Florida State University on November 29, 1993, by the Florida Board of Regents, and took office on January 3, 1994. His grandfather attended the Seminary West of the Suwannee and his mother attended Florida State College for Women, giving him a long personal legacy with the institution that eventually became FSU. ¶ His presidency has been marked by enthusiasm, energy, ideas, and a holistic vision for FSU that encompasses telling details (such as landscaping and campus driving) and grand designs (such as an ambitious arts festival and a new College of Medicine). D'Alemberte took into its sesquicentennial year a university of remarkable prowess and promise not only in sports but in arts and the sciences, both social and natural, theoretical and applied. ¶ Two achievements can perhaps stand as emblems for FSU's entry, with strength and maturity, into the twenty-first century: the Taxol-synthesis process invented by chemistry professor Dr. Robert Holton and the establishment of the eminent Eppes Professorships. Dr. Holton's discovery not only changed the lives of cancer sufferers and their families worldwide— by making the revolutionary anticancer agent available and affordable—but its royalty income fueled more research and improved programs university-wide. The bold idea of enticing and hiring Eppes Professors—'super professors' preeminent in their fields—was in part made possible by Dr. Holton and his research team. ¶ Florida State University, on its 150th birthday in 2001, is what higher education should be: a source of discoveries igniting an unending chain reaction of public service, teaching, scholarship, and creativity.

Talbot (Sandy) D'Alemberte, President, 1994 – Present

Born June 1, 1933, in Tallahassee, Sandy D'Alemberte was educated in public schools in Tallahassee and Chattahoochee, Florida. In 1955 he earned his bachelor of arts degree with honors in political science from the University of the South in Suwannee and also attended summer school at FSU and the University of Virginia. In 1962 he received his juris doctor with honors from the University of Florida.

D'Alemberte practiced law with the Steel Hector & Davis firm in Miami and Tallahassee, where he began his legal career in 1962. He was named partner in 1965. An active member of many legal and higher educational organizations, he was the 1991–1992 president of the American Bar Association and the 1982–1984 president of the American Judicature Society.

D'Alemberte represented Dade County in the Florida House of Representatives from 1966 to 1972 and chaired several legislative committees. After leaving the Florida Legislature he chaired the Florida Commission on Ethics and the Florida Constitution Revision Commission.

An educator and author as well, D'Alemberte served as the fourth dean of the FSU College of Law (1984–1989) and continues to teach as a member of the university faculty. His book *The Florida Constitution* was published by Greenwood Press in 1991. He also coedited the 1990 four-volume work *The Florida Civil Trial Guide* and has published over twenty articles.

D'Alemberte is married to Patsy Palmer, former children's policy coordinator in Florida Governor Lawton Chiles' office. She has been a journalist, legislative aide, and White House staff member.

Below: Playing in honor of FSU's first Seven Days of Opening Nights Arts Festival, Sandy D'Alemberte, Winston Scott, and Bobby Bowden, 1999

Opposite: President D'Alemberte and his wife, Patsy Palmer, on a bicycle built for two, homecoming parade, 1996

*"Sandy and I both care enormously about our community and showing off
what the university can and will be."*

PATSY PALMER

On sixty acres on Sarasota Bay is the John and Mable Ringling Museum of Art, with one of the most valuable collections in the nation, a circus museum, and a thirty-one-room Venetian-style mansion. On July 1, 2001, the Legislature voted to transfer the Ringling from Florida's Department of State to Florida State University.

FSU will administer Cà d 'Zan, the former Ringling home, and use it for education—from the elementary-school through university levels. The FSU Center for the Fine and Performing Arts will conduct academic programs in theatre, dance, art, art history and museum management.

The museum was willed to the state by John Ringling, who died in 1936. The Legislature has given FSU possession of the Ringling collection and authority to administer the land and buildings. The governor and the cabinet will continue to hold title to the property.

The collection includes major works by Peter Paul Rubens, Diego Velasquez and Rosa Bonheur. The museum specializes in Baroque art but its collection also includes antiquities, sculpture, and decorative arts.

The Appleton Museum of Art in Ocala is one of the South's premier art repositories and education centers. Originally built to display and preserve the collection of Arthur I. Appleton, the museum has expanded to include traveling exhibitions, educational programs, and cultural events.

The museum is the focal point of the Appleton Cultural Center, a 44-acre complex which also includes the Ocala Civic Theatre and the Pioneer Garden Club. The museum building is a contemporary interpretation of classical architecture clad in travertine marble. Sitting on 11.3 wooded and landscaped acres, it commands a small rise preceded by a cascading marble reflecting pool and fountain.

The Museum is the realization of a dream of Arthur I. Appleton, retired president of Appleton Electric Company of Chicago, avid art collector, and owner of Bridlewood Farm, a Marion County thoroughbred operation. Appleton, together with a group of community leaders, persuaded the city of Ocala to donate land for the museum. Arthur, his wife Martha, and his sister Edith-Marie Appleton donated funds to build the museum structure. The museum opened to the public in December 1987. Since July 1, 1990, the Appleton Museum of Art has been jointly owned by Florida State University and Central Florida Community College.

Susan Baldino, Director of Appleton Programs and Museum

I left the metropolitan areas of New York and Atlanta for Tallahassee, wondering what I had gotten myself into. Tallahassee was sultry and beautiful in its own way, the people I met were friendly and, although it was tough to find a downtown restaurant open for Saturday lunch, I discovered lots of interesting places to go and things to do. It didn't take me long to figure out that I wanted to take advantage of the most precious resource in town: Florida State University. I decided to return to college life for graduate study.

My field was art history. From prehistoric cave painting to contemporary installation, I loved art of all kinds. Worried that I would be labeled a dilettante, I tried very hard to concentrate on certain aspects of Baroque architecture, but it was the entire history of art that was my true love. I felt better after I divulged my overarching affection for the discipline to Pat Rose, chair of art history at the time. Pat was, and still is, the person I hold in highest regard. She told me that she was afflicted with the same passion, that she couldn't claim any one area in the history of art as her unequivocal favorite. Satisfied that I felt the same way as my mentor and idol, I continued to soak in information about all the different methodologies, movements, and media.

After my classes were over, my exams taken and thesis written, I moved on to become not only a proud alum, but part of FSU's administrative staff. It thrills me to think that I have the opportunity to remain in academe, surrounded by the wealth of knowledge that first attracted me to the university, helping to develop educational programs for students. I came on board when Arthur Appleton conferred to FSU the university's largest single gift, which included the Appleton Museum of Art and associated endowments. The past few years of working with art and artifacts in the museum context and interfacing with Appleton Eminent Scholars of world renown have been my greatest professional joys. With the advent of museum studies, a graduate certificate program for students who want museum careers, and the acquisition of the John and Mable Ringling Museum of Art, I feel that I am in the right place at the right time. This university has made a commitment to the arts and to museums, and I take great pleasure in joining my colleagues that have made this happen.

Left: *The Triumph of Divine Love* (c. 1625) by Peter Paul Rubens (1577–1640) and studio is just one of the many important paintings in the collection of the John and Mable Ringling Museum of Art, the state art museum of Florida.

Right: Cà d 'Zan (1924–1926), the Ringling winter residence, west façade from Sarasota Bay

Named after one of FSU's most prominent founding fathers, the Francis Eppes Professorships were begun in 1999. Funded by the FSU Research Foundation using profits from the interest generated by royalties, they are designed to recruit "super professors." "We are delighted with the standard established thus far with our Eppes Professors," says FSU President Talbot (Sandy) D'Alemberte. Included in this distinguished group are the following:

Charles McClure, an expert in electronic communication. McClure directs a new institute that researches the Internet's effectiveness for information and for commerce.

In 1983 FSU alumna **Ellen Taaffe Zwilich** was the first woman to receive a Pulitzer Prize for music composition, for her Symphony No. 1. She has held the Carnegie Hall Composer's Chair since 1995.

For more than twenty years, **Gerald R. Ferris** has studied the influence of politics and interpersonal relationships on workplace hiring, job evaluation, and promotion.

Leonard (Chick) LaPointe, hailed by the American Speech-Hearing-Language Association as a visionary in communication disorders, has joined the communication disorders department. LaPointe founded and edits *The Journal of Medical Speech-Language Pathology*.

Robert Olen Butler comes to the creative writing program from McNeese State University. A 1993 Pulitzer Prize winner for his collection of stories *A Good Scent from a Strange Mountain*, Butler brings his talents to both graduate and undergraduate English students.

Suzanne Farrell, School of Visual Arts and Dance, was muse to the great George Balanchine. Known throughout the world as the inspiration and prima ballerina of many of Balanchine's greatest ballets, Farrell retired from the stage in 1989. The John F. Kennedy Center for the Performing Arts is the host institution for her acclaimed dance company and for her intensive courses for young dancers.

John Scholz is a political scientist whose research focuses on politics, administration, and public policy with an emphasis on political economy and institutions, organization and decision theory, citizenship and taxes, and government regulation of business.

Advancing the study of biology at FSU is **David Swofford**, one of the world's leading experts in phylogenics, the study of the evolutionary relationships among organisms. One of Swofford's achievements is developing software for scientists to use in analyzing DNA sequences.

Jane Alexander, an actress and arts activist, has been appointed an Eppes Professor in Theatre. Chairman of the National Endowment for the Arts from 1993 to 1997, she has won an Emmy, a Tony and four Academy Award nominations. Her latest film, *Sunshine State*, celebrates her new home base.

Barrett Hathcock, FSU Media Relations

Opposite top: Robert Olen Butler,
Eppes Professor of English

Opposite bottom: Ellen Taaffe Zwilich,
Eppes Professor of Music

"*I tell my writing students that works of art do not come from the mind, they come from the place where you dream. I deeply believe that.*"

ROBERT OLEN BUTLER

College of Medicine

Florida State's spanking new medical school was off and running in 2001, with Dr. Joseph E. Scherger from the University of California Irvine's College of Medicine tapped as dean of the new school. By any measure, Scherger, fifty, appears to be a fine fit for the startup program, the first medical school of its kind to open in twenty years. Created to supply rural and underserved areas of Florida with physicians trained in geriatric and primary care, the new school stands to get a jump-start from Scherger's experience and personal interests.

Scherger's career as an educator reflects a strong bent toward serving the elderly and revamping the way this country distributes health care.

Scherger greeted the charter class of thirty students on the school's opening day, May 7. "Patients deserve the best care no matter where they live, even in the small towns in the Panhandle," Scherger told his audience.

All of the school's students are from Florida, and at least a third of them come from small hometowns. Ninety percent of the students say they are pursuing careers in primary care or general practice medicine. They are on track to graduate in 2005.

College of Social Sciences

Founded in 1973, the College of Social Sciences has been educating students in the ways of the world for almost thirty years. Professors and students alike have studied how people govern themselves, interact with others and the environment, and plan their surroundings.

Marie Cowart, dean of the college, is known for her research in public health policy and in recent years has been involved in research on elder care and social services conducted at the FSU Pepper Institute on Aging and Public Policy named after Senator Claude Pepper. She was the institute's director from 1985 to 1992.

Phyllis Allsopp Ward (class of 1949)

My fellow FSU art students of the years 1948 and 1949 may not have been as lucky as I was to have stumbled onto a news story about us. We not only took art history, we made art history!

Visiting Sarasota in 1994 I was dumbstruck to see an old photograph in the morning paper of a group of FSU art students (including myself) taken in the Ringling Museum while we were attending an art seminar in April 1948. It was the same photo that had appeared in the *Tally Ho Forty Niner*, the FSU yearbook.

The *Sarasota Herald Tribune* I saw was heralding a historic 1948 art show put together by the first director of the Ringling Museum, A. Everett Austin, Jr. (called Chick). Mrs. Beatrice Williams was head of the FSU Art Department at that time and deserves credit for having the courage and fortitude to chaperone eighteen young people, mostly girls, for three weeks for this marvelous experience.

Artemis Skevakis (Housewright), who painted the mural in Dodd Hall that commemorates the class of 1949–1950, was a participant in this art seminar, as well as editor of the *Tally Ho Forty Niner*.

The Institute on Napoleon and the French Revolution, Department of History, is under the direction of Donald Horward. Started in 1961 with fewer than 20 volumes, the French Revolution and Napoleon collection of the Strozier Library now includes over 18,000 titles.

The FSU Institute on World War II and the Human Experience, supervised by William O. Oldson, Department of History, focuses on preserving the memories and artifacts of WWII servicemen and women and of civilians who helped on the home front.

The Master Craftsman Program, under the direction of Bob Bischoff, was conceived as a means of creating an awareness of what constitutes a finely crafted object and teaching the skills and professionalism to fabricate the objects.

Chemistry professor Robert A. Holton and his research group have become world renowned for their work in synthesizing Taxol—one of the most successful cancer drugs of the twentieth century. Taxol, occurring naturally in scarce pacific Yew trees, has extended and saved thousands of lives and has generated hundreds of millions of dollars in royalties for FSU, money reinvested in research and educational programs. In fact, a portion of these royalties has helped Holton's team develop a whole new class of taxol analog drugs that offer even more promise than Taxol.

The Taxol story strongly demonstrates the value of scientific research. However, according to Dr. Michael D. Devine, associate vice-president for research at FSU from 1987 to 1995, less well known is the role that luck and just plain hard work play in such accomplishments. He should know. In 1990 Devine worked hand-in-hand for eight months with Holton negotiating the patent license agreement with Bristol Myers Squibb. He continued to work with Holton almost daily on licensing issues until he left FSU in 1995, only to return in 2000 to head Holton's MDS (Molecular Design and Synthesis) Research Foundation.

"Bob Holton is a brilliant scientist, no doubt about it," says Devine, "but without a lot of luck, and without Holton's steadfast refusal to let roadblocks stop his goals, none of this would have happened." As just one example, in the early 90s Bristol was evaluating many options to supply large quantities of Taxol from some source other than the endangered yew trees. Any number of corporate decisions could have led away from the Holton process. In fact, the patented process that FSU originally licensed to Bristol was not the one the company commercialized; Bristol used an improved process that Holton later invented.

As another example, Bristol almost used the original license agreement to block further development of taxol analogs. Only by long, difficult, never-say-die negotiation on Holton's and FSU's part was a settlement reached to allow the new research to go forward. Today, one of the analogs already has reached crucial clinical trials—but only because of Holton's tireless efforts in spearheading the nonprofit MDS Research Foundation and the for-profit company Taxolog, which speeds rigorous testing. "Without a doubt," concludes Devine, "none of these milestones would have been reached if the same science had been developed by a less-committed individual."

Robert Holton, FSU organic chemist, holds a model of the molecular structure of taxol in 1993. Thanks to Holton's work, FSU holds the patent on the synthesis of this important anti-cancer drug.

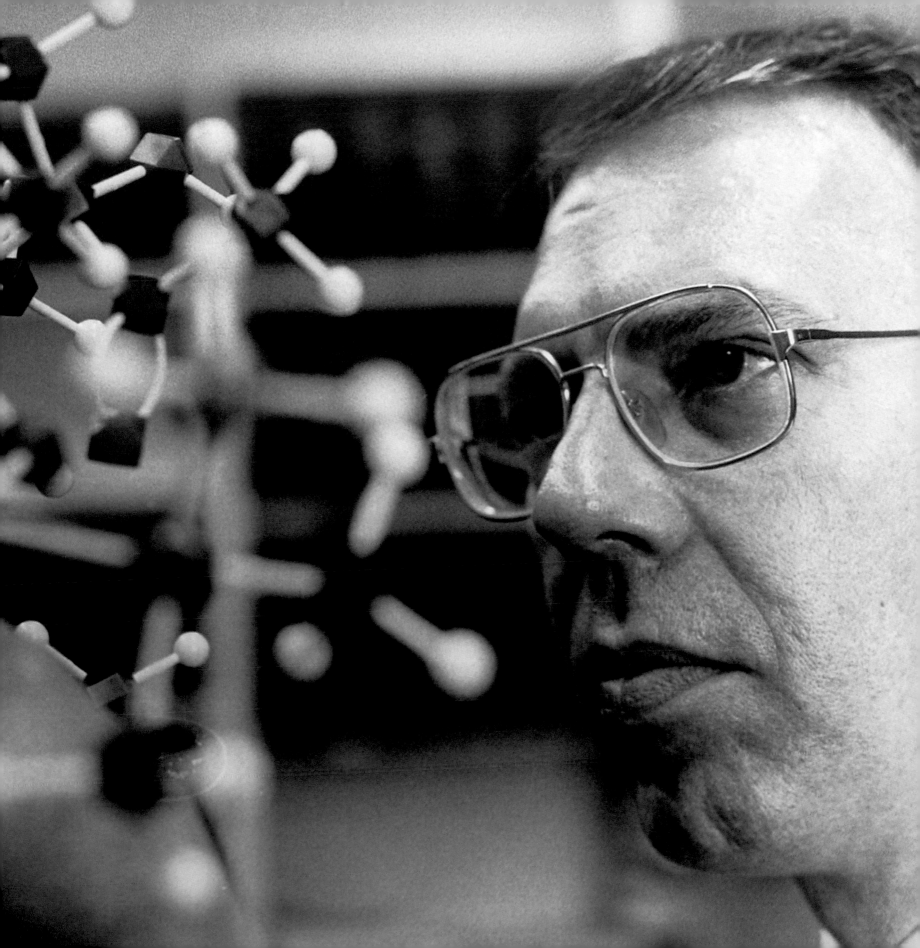

The Beginning: On January 23, 1915, the first issue of the *Florida Flambeau* appeared. According to Ruby Leach, class of 1915 and the newspaper's first editor, she had complained to Milton Smith, editor of the *Tallahassee Democrat*, about the sparseness of college news in his paper. He hired her to write two columns per week about campus activities at fifty cents per column. When the faculty realized from Leach's columns that the college had enough activities to warrant a newspaper, President Conradi presented the idea to the students, who agreed. Student Lucille Freeman proposed the publication's name: she simply took a dictionary and ran her fingers slowly down the f's until she came to *flambeau*, a flaming torch.

Faculty sponsors passed judgment on all student publications, and the *Flambeau* never dared to challenge the administration until after World War I. Just as the Student Government Association gained strength and focus from wartime, so the paper evinced more student concerns and campus problems.

By 1920, an editorial boldly challenged the faculty's habit of skipping required chapel services. It asked, "Where are the professors in chapel? We meet every day at 12:00 noon in the auditorium for a few minutes of devotion, yet a majority of the teachers are conspicuous for their absence."

The Middle Years: In the early 1960s *Flambeau* editor Virginia Delavan voiced strong support for the efforts of Tallahassee blacks to integrate Woolworth's lunch counter, leading to her arrest during a protest downtown.

Not all issues were this serious, however. Rick Johnson, former general manager of the *Flambeau* and involved with the paper since 1965 when he was a runner (carrying copy from the newsroom to the lab), said "Some of the issues we were dealing with then would seem laughable now, such as whether women would be allowed to wear pants on campus."

Until 1972 the *Flambeau* was largely financed by the university to the tune of $150,000 a year, with a small percentage of income generated by advertising fees. By 1980 the paper had a daily readership of over 40,000 but some serious problems. Many factors led to the *Flambeau*'s being pushed out to survive on its own. One was editorial censorship by university presidents John Champion and Stanley Marshall.

"Typically any editorial that stated an opinion critical of the administration would be sent back and revised," said Johnson. "Some of the editors took to running a space where the editorial would go with just the word *censored*."

As president, Marshall was publisher of all student publications. After a number of censorship cases, Attorney General Bob Shevin ruled that the First Amendment prohibited the president from censoring the newspaper. Marshall felt that this left him in an untenable position: being held accountable for the *Flambeau*'s words but having no control over them.

Independence: Increased criticism of the administration resulted in a decree handed down in April of 1972: the *Flambeau* had six months before all university funding, at this time more than half of all operating costs, would be cut off.

The *Flambeau* staff girded themselves that first year as an independent business and lost $9,000. "A lot of people worked for nothing," recalled Johnson, "but there was enough anger to keep us going for two years." The *Flambeau* showed a profit that second year. It was clear from the beginning, however, that the paper did not have the financial cushion it needed and, said Johnson, "All it would take is one bad year for our life to end."

Meanwhile the paper was widely read and committed to quality. In 1979 Gerald Ensley won *Sports Illustrated*'s College Sportswriting Award for his work on the paper. Not long after, the *Flambeau* turned a self-critical eye on its own practices.

Ironically the *Flambeau*'s liberal following in the '80s brought them to task on the issue of women's representation on the paper. While the business staff was predominately female, the editorial side lacked women writers. Both general manager Rick Johnson and editor Sidney Bedingfield agreed with the criticism and initiated an affirmative action policy. For the next decade, the editors worked to broaden their coverage of minority issues, do more investigative journalism, improve the over-all quality of the paper, and hire writers with more experience.

The End: The *Florida Flambeau* continued to wage journalistic war on the status quo until the late 1990s when because of financial difficulties it was bought by and merged with a newer publication on campus, *FSView*.

Sources: Robin Jeanne Sellers, *Femina Perfecta*, 1995, and Ira Shorr, *Florida State*, Summer 1980

Prior to his cartoon days, Bud Grace, Ph.D. 1971, taught physics and did research. In 1979 he left science and began cartooning professionally. His comic strip *Ernie*, also called *The Piranha Club*, began in 1988 and now appears in nearly 400 papers.

For her internationally recognized research in ecology and evolutionary biology, oceanography professor Nancy H. Marcus was named FSU's Robert O. Lawton Distinguished Professor for 2001–2002. Marcus, the director of the FSU Marine Laboratory since 1989, is an innovative and highly influential zooplankton ecologist, internationally recognized as one of the leading biological oceanographers in the country. She was elected president of the American Society of Limnologists and Oceanographers and to the Ocean Studies Board of the National Academy of Sciences. Marcus has also done much to attract young people to the sciences.

At the award ceremony Marcus paid tribute to the many women scientists, the "true pioneers" she called her "scientific ancestors" at Florida State. They ranged from Elizabeth Bangs, the first woman to teach science at the Seminary West of the Suwannee River, 1893–1900 (and who was paid $900 a year), to Margaret Menzel, who came to FSU in 1955 with her husband Winston, also a professor. Marcus noted that

> *Margaret Menzel is remembered as an accomplished botanist and geneticist who also fought for the rights of women. In 1971 she founded the local chapter of the National Organization for Women (NOW). In 1972 she spearheaded a class action suit against FSU to rectify the lower salaries for faculty women compared to men. The suit included five other women faculty members. They won the suit and were awarded back pay. . . .Currently the FSU Department of Biological Sciences awards the Margaret Menzel Award each year to a biology graduate student for outstanding progress in research.*

Nancy Marcus, Professor of Oceanography, was the 2001–02 Robert O. Lawton Distinguished Professor.

Top: Harold Knowles is managing shareholder with the firm of Knowles, Marks & Randolph, P.A., Tallahassee, the oldest African-American law firm in North Florida, and a trustee, FSU Board of Trustees. He received his bachelor's degree from FSU in 1970 and his law degree from the FSU College of Law in 1973.

Bottom: Paula Fortunas began her career at the Florida State University Foundation in 1964 as a student assistant and went on to be a graduate assistant and then full-time business manager. In 1975 she was named director of finance and accounting and in 1987 became vice-president for planned giving. In 2000 she received the Quarter-Century Award given by the Council for the Advancement and Support of Education (CASE) which recognizes lifetime achievement among development professionals.

Steven J. Uhlfelder, Florida State University Trustee

It is hard to imagine that as former student body president of the University of Florida I would care as much about Florida State University as I do. All of the special women in my life attended this wonderful place. My mom went to Florida State College for Women. Because of the war, she never graduated but met my dad, who was working in Tallahassee. My wife, Miffie, received her master of fine arts at FSU, and my daughter, Ali, graduated from FSU with a degree in social science. I even had the honor as chairman of the Board of Regents to give the commencement address at my daughter's graduation.

In addition to my family connections, many special circumstances link me to the campus. During my tenure as student body president at Florida, I became friends with FSU president Stanley Marshall and student body president Chuck Sherman. I also met then-legislator Sandy D'Alemberte, who took a special interest in me and has remained a very close friend and mentor for over thirty years.

But as important as the personal reasons are, I have more substantive ones for appreciating FSU. Over the twenty-six years that I have lived in Tallahassee, I have observed the crucial role it plays in our community. It has made my life here much more meaningful. The university is a caring place, promotes community service, and encourages diversity of opinions and ideas. Two wonderful examples are the Southside Initiative and the Holocaust Teacher Training Institute. The Southside Initiative provides resources, support, and expertise to our at-risk public schools in Tallahassee and sets a great example for others to follow. Many children now have mentors and role models who would be missing in their lives without FSU's efforts. The Holocaust Institute offers a week-long course for high school teachers about the Holocaust and its many lessons. Without this preparation for teachers, many of our students would never be exposed to this horrendous history. I have been honored to be a part of both programs.

Steven J. Uhlfelder, president of Uhlfelder and Associates law firm, is a member of the FSU Board of Trustees.

Jon R. Piersol, Dean and Professor, School of Music

Jon R. Piersol has been dean of the School of Music since 1991. Offering one of the finest programs in the country, the school, with more than 80 faculty members, enrolls over 650 undergraduate and 350 graduate students.

It's hard to miss some of the class gifts on campus. Two good examples are the Westcott fountain, given by the classes of 1915 and 1917, and the iron arch leading to it, given by the classes of 1916 and 1918.

These gifts started to grace the campus in 1910 in the form of two bas-reliefs for the walls of the browsing room in the library. Since then they have included: scholarships, student loans, and buildings. Twelve classes contributed to the construction and furnishing of the Longmire building, completed in 1937. Over the years, classes have given pianos, bronze doors for Westcott, the sun dial in front of Bryan Hall, furniture, and chimes.

Recently, some classes have come back to give a second gift, perhaps as a celebration of 50 years as graduates or as a 150th birthday present.

The classes of 1949 and 1950 gave a 50th anniversary gift of a mural, installed in Dodd Hall, painted by Artemis Housewright, a well-known southern painter.

The transition classes of FSCW 1946, FSCW/FSU 1947, and FSU 1948 gave the Heritage Tower, a solid brick structure across from Doak Campbell Stadium, as their 50th anniversary gift. And the class of 1944 presented a valuable 150th birthday present: a rare 1829 map of the Florida territory. Though new graduates are less able to buy expensive presents than the long-employed, the class of 1994 raised enough money to install the clock and seal high atop the University Center. The clock and seal, visible across Pensacola Street from the Heritage Tower, are already familiar sights to students and Tallahasseeans.

"I remember helping to raise money for the clock and seal as a student," said Robin Kimbrough Haggins. "I still have the T-shirt we were selling for that project."

Haggins is now deeply involved with class gifts as the director of development for student affairs. "The class of 1999 decided on a stained glass window, which was recently installed in the Student Life Building," she said. "The idea of the window is to showcase student life on campus, and it's really beautiful."

The 2000 graduates got their project installed in record time. They decided on three seals depicting the beginning of the institution—where Westcott now stands—until today. The class of 2001 is doing a joint project with the class of 1951, the class of former Gov. Reubin Askew, who is now a professor and eminent scholar in FSU's Askew School of Public Administration and Policy. They'll work together in refurbishing Landis Green and its fountain.

"We want every graduating class from here on out to sponsor a gift, a lasting legacy," Haggins said. "It will always be especially meaningful for them."

Bayard Stern, *Florida State Times*, October 2001

William Anthony, Carl DeSantis Professor of Business Administration and Director of the Carl DeSantis Center for Executive Management Education

I left Ohio State University in Columbus for my interview at Florida State on a dark gray February day. When I returned two days later, my car was encrusted with a layer of ice. I could not open the doors! What a contrast to the mid-70 degree weather I had experienced in Florida! The weather was important, but that is not what sold me on the school. FSU had the complete package. A major university in a state capital with a superb faculty, a Ph.D. program in my area, a great football team—and great weather to boot!

When I told my wife that I thought I would accept the job, she said "We are going where?" I gave her Gloria Jahoda's book to read, *The Other Florida*. She said, "Oh well, I guess we can put up with it for two years." That was thirty-two years ago.

T.N. Krishnamurti, Department of Meteorology

World-renowned meteorologist T.N. Krishnamurti has developed a method of hurricane forecasting that combines multiple forecasting models and reduces built-in errors or biases. The result is an ensemble of models—a "superensemble"—that combines the best aspects of the sum of its parts and produces as close to a bias-free forecast as exists. In 1999, Krishnamurti reported a 20–30% improvement overall in his own forecasting and up to 100% in other models using the technique.

Krishnamurti's research drew national attention when his superensemble technique produced a prediction, for the path of Hurricane Floyd and other storms of 1999, with fewer track errors than all of the participating models.

Given enough computing power, Krishnamurti says the model could be applied to everyday weather analysis, a prospect that could make newscasts' six-day forecasts much more dependable. "Krish," as he's known to friends and colleagues around the world, has received many accolades throughout his career, including FSU's Lawton Professorship and the Carl Gustaf Rossby Research Medal, the highest award given by the American Meteorological Society. His research has been supported by NOAA, NASA, and the National Science Foundation.

FSU Office of Research, *Annual Report*, 2000

President Sandy D'Alemberte escorts Rosa Parks, who was awarded an honorary degree for her work in civil rights, 1995.

Reubin O. Askew

In 1951, the year Reubin Askew received his B.A. degree in public administration from FSU, he was president of the Student Government Association and a member of ODK and Gold Key (not to mention king of the prom).

From 1971 to 1979 Askew was the governor of Florida and afterward served as the United States Trade Representative during the second half of President Jimmy Carter's term, from 1979 to 1980.

Today Reubin Askew is a distinguished professor of public policy at the Askew School of Public Administration and Policy, Florida State University, as well as a senior fellow with the Florida Institute of Government and of counsel to Akerman, Senterfitt & Eidson, PA.

Reubin O. Askew,
Governor of Florida,
1971–1979

Ed Love, Professor of Art

Peace, Goodwill, and Ed Love

Ed Love, a sculptor and professor of art, died suddenly in 1999. Virgil Suarez, a professor of English and a poet, wrote this celebration of Love and his life.

Ed Love was a good friend of mine. More than that, Ed became a mentor to me over the time I knew him here in Tallahassee. I liked to visit his studio in Railroad Square frequently because, as I told Ed many times, I found a spiritual energy there that he had harnessed in his own work.

It was in the work that Ed Love found peace, found courage, found energy and I found it for my own poetry there. He knew it because I had told him, but many times I merely went to soak it up; whatever Ed was coaxing out of his metal scraps, I wanted to bring out of my blank pieces of paper. It was about the daily work, he often said to me, the routine, the picking up where you left off the day before.

I had found in Ed's company and teachings a way to approach my own work, and I think so far it's paid off. I'm going to miss Ed Love, the person, the teacher, as I am sure hundreds of his students will. *En pace requiescat, amigo*.

Virgil Suarez, *Research in Review*, Summer 1999

Diane K. Roberts: Pigskin Pleasures

Diane Roberts, Ph.D., is a commentator for National Public Radio and teaches at the University of Alabama, Tuscaloosa.

When I was nine, my father died and I inherited his Florida State Seminoles football season tickets. This was in the late '60s and people—Southern people, anyway—dressed properly for games: coat and tie, Chanel-copy suits, spike heels, matching lizard bags, pillbox hats, and cabbage-size corsages. Just what you'd wear for church. This was no coincidence. It was part of people's—Southern people's—understanding of the sacred.

I have a day job as an academic, a feminist scholar, even. I know how to officially disapprove of college football, to talk about how it drains attention and resources from the educational imperative of the university, how it breeds violence, bolsters the most extreme gender roles, and rewards a scary combination of illiteracy, thuggishness and authoritarianism. I know a lot of bad stuff about sex, chocolate and the Democratic Party, too. None of it has stopped me yet. I am a stone college football fan.

I was at early FSU vs. University of Florida games; the Gators had stickers on their helmets that read "Never, FSU, Never." I was at the Pittsburgh game when a November hurricane squatted in the Gulf; it rained so viciously we couldn't see the ball from the stands. You don't leave a football game just because there's a life-and-property-threatening weather system a few miles away.

And you don't leave a football game just because your team is losing by four touchdowns. I sat through the 0–11 and 1–10 seasons in the '70s. That kind of pain purifies the soul, like the Bible says. Also, it was perversely fun. You could go berserk with joy over a field goal. Being a serious college football fan is like choosing to be a manic depressive: exciting but not always healthy.

But you were a Seminole, you spent Saturday afternoons eating cold ham and chicken and sitting in long lines of traffic and fretting over the lack of depth in the secondary. You sang the fight song and the "Hymn to the Garnet and Gold," and you hollered the most complicated cheers, knowing the words for Saturday afternoon better than you knew the words for the doxology and the Apostle's Creed on Sunday morning.

Now, of course, people put on any old thing for church and they wear T-shirts with feathers glued to them to football games. But that satisfying, if retrograde, spiritual football pleasure is the same. Team allegiance is a most fundamental mark of identity.

The University of Florida was always the elite college in my state. Boys from the old cotton and peanut farming families in west Florida came down to pledge KA or SAE; boys from the new money of real estate or orange juice or phosphate came up to participate in the Florida that was still the South. The school song was "We Are the Boys from Old Florida" and used always to be played with a few bars of "Dixie" embedded in it, just to underscore the way the University of Florida represented who was in charge and what was what in all matters racial, sexual, economic and social.

Florida State used to be the women's college: underfunded, patrolled by fierce old lady deans and stiff with rules about the wearing of shorts and staying out after 10 p.m. But in 1947, Florida State College for Women became Florida State University and admitted men—who took about 30 seconds to institute the playing of football. FSU began squaring up against the tiny-college likes of Furman, Millsaps and the Citadel. The University of Florida refused to play FSU. You don't play football against girls.

Eventually the Florida Legislature forced the snooty Gators to meet the Seminoles. For UF to play FSU was an act of *lèse-majesté*, like making the United States Senate play strip poker against the Capitol Hill cleaning ladies.

"Never, FSU, Never," the Florida fans always said. We FSU fans said—sometimes sang— "Go to Hell, Gators, go to Hell." I loved that. I grew up in a house where children and women did not utter profanity. "Darn" was thought to be at the edge of unseemly. "Dadgummit" was pushing it. But I was allowed to say "hell" when addressing the University of Florida. It was, after all, a genuine theologial sentiment.

Diane Roberts, *Atlanta Journal-Constitution*, November 3, 1996

Catherine Lewis (Ph.D., English, 1996)

I paid my way through graduate school at FSU by working as a police officer for the city of Tallahassee. The best overtime shift to pick up was a home football game. I was often assigned to crowd control inside the stadium, where I was able to witness some great plays in between giving directions and ejecting the occasional drunk (always from the other team). I'd leave the last few minutes of the game in order to be at my traffic post when the thousands of cars came streaming out of the stadium.

Outside I'd see the protesters, orderly, yet vocal, with their signs objecting to the Seminole Indian portrayal. Most people ignored them. Some cursed them. After all, who could deny the thrill and hoopla of watching a painted Seminole chief thrust his spear into the heart of the ball field? I switched the moccasin to my own cultural foot while walking to my traffic post. I imagined a short green Irishman out there staggering drunkenly and throwing coins from a pot of gold—one of which must have fallen into my shoe because suddenly it didn't feel so comfortable.

The game ended. Our tribe had won and the stampede of traffic ensued. We moved hundreds of cars in minutes. Traffic control is down to a science. Though there is always one renegade, usually driving a you-know-what (if you don't know, it's probably because you drive one of them) that breaks away, cutting off the herd and causing screeched halts and long honks, all to escape a minute or two of waiting. This time, though, I catch him, pull him over, and take his license. "Sir," I say, "didn't you see that arrow back there?"

"Arrow?" he says. "Hell, I didn't even see the Indian."

I laughed and then, I'll leave you wondering if he got a ticket.

Left: Peter Warrick, now in NFL, reaching for a pass in 1999

Right: The National Championship football team presents President William Clinton with an FSU jersey, March 2, 2000. FSU was the first sports team Clinton received as president of the U.S., in the winter of 1994.

"After we won the 1966 Florida football game, we rushed the field and picked grass to keep as souvenirs. The grass is still in my scrapbook."

MELISSA LINTZ (CLASS OF 2000)

192

"I was Chief Osceola during the 1999 national championship season. The excitement and the honor of being the symbol of the Florida State University Seminole football team is a memory I will never forget."

DANIEL KENNERLY (CLASS OF 2001)

Daniel Kennerly as Chief Osceola on Renegade

"In November 1996, my wife Rachel and friends camped out from Friday to Monday morning with about 2,000 other students at the stadium waiting for UF/FSU tickets. We stayed in a tent with our dogs in 35 degree weather."

AARON J. SOLOMON (CLASS OF 1997)

Robin Nigh

How important are the formative years for kids in their perception of education and sports? Some of the happiest memories I share with my dad are listening to the Gator games on the radio. I remember driving home to south Florida from visiting family in Tallahassee and hearing the Gators blow it in the final minutes of the Florida/Georgia game. I remember listening to the Florida/FSU games on the radio after the yard was mowed, the grill was warming up for dinner, and the FSU players were running into the stadium. I went on to UF to receive my B.F.A.

Fast forward fifteen years. I have children, and ironically, I am living in Tallahassee and pursuing my Ph.D. at FSU. How familiar and strange it is to me that my children's fondest memories will be when they went to the games with their dad (while mom studied).

We have since moved, but my children's unwavering support for the Seminoles continues. The most recent show of fan support came from my eldest, Dylan, who just got braces. Did you know they come in colors now? Well, imagine my surprise when he comes home from his first trip to the orthodontist with garnet and gold bands!

David Hart, Jr., Director of
Intercollegiate Athletics

Mike Futrell at bat in game against
University of Florida, 1999

Coach Mike Martin celebrates his 1000th victory, April 8, 1998. The win was 4–3 over Jacksonville University. Mike Martin played baseball with Dick Howser while both were students at FSU. When Howser left in 1980 to manage the New York Yankees Martin became a successful and popular head coach.

FSU softball coach JoAnne Graf's 1000th victory, 6-4 vs. the University of South Florida, May 6, 1999

Sarah Elizabeth Scobey (class of 2000)

I would have to say my most memorable experience at FSU was being on the swim team. I will never forget the mornings at 6:00 a.m. when it was freezing cold outside and the pool was warm from the heaters. It would be cold outside and still dark. There would be a fog hovering over the pool, and it was difficult to see the swimmers in the fog. But I loved thinking about all the students still asleep in the dorms and apartments surrounding the school. There were times I wished I was still asleep in the comfort of my bed. But looking back on it, I wouldn't have given up a single morning practice to sleep in every morning of my four years at FSU. Competing at FSU on a varsity team is the one thing I am still most proud of today, and I know I'll always hold that memory dear to me.

Cecelia Maloney (M.A. 1974)

Around 1974 and 1975 a group of us would go to the football games—at any time during the game—and sit on the 50 yard line—not many people went to the games then. Coach Darrell Mudra used to sit up in the press box, not on the field, and watch the game. The cheerleaders at that time had the strangest cheers. They would shout "Pursue! Endeavor!"

Pat Seery, who started the Grassroots Free School in Tallahassee in 1975, used to sell peanuts at all the games. That way he got in for free. He had his own sales strategy: He'd follow the ball—whatever yard the ball was on, that's where Pat would sell his peanuts. Then, late at night, every night, Pat would go to Chanelo's to eat any pizzas that weren't delivered. They expected him—he'd do a little cleaning to help out. If they didn't have any leftover pizza, they'd make him one!

Opposite: Marvin (Snoop) Minnis and Chris Weinke celebrate a
30–23 win over University of Florida in 1999—next step,
the Sugar Bowl.

Bottom left: "March Madness," women's NCAA tournament vs.
Iowa State. Brooke Wyckoff, #21, was named team MVP for
women's basketball in 2001.

Top right: Coach Bobby Bowden holding trophy won in 1990
Sugar Bowl against Virginia Tech

Center right: Peter Tom Willis (L) and Gene Deckerhoff, FSU
radio team, 1998

Bottom right: April Murphy, first soccer scrimmage in 1999
under new head coach, Patrick Baker

"Remember Mercury, the Roman god of merchandise and merchants, cleverness, and speed? Wings on his feet propelled him to adventures far and wide. Rest assured, his spirit lives on in my department. In recent years, computers have taken hold and students and faculty find themselves going to Asia, Australia, and all points European. But at the end of the day, we slip off our flying shoes, reflect, and realize how far we have come, grateful to be part of this great university, and, then, we dream of things to come."

ELIZABETH GOLDSMITH, PROFESSOR, DEPARTMENT OF TEXTILES AND CONSUMER SCIENCES (CLASS OF 1971)

Jane Robbins, Dean of the School of Information Studies, does her part during "Dunk the Dean" festivities at the school.

Boys' Choir Singers Are "Coming Up Taller"

The boys' choir began when Dianne Harrison Montgomery, who was then dean of the FSU School of Social Work, and Professor Gerald O'Conner asked Earle Lee, a social work professor in South Carolina, to bring to FSU his idea of inspiring underachieving black males through music.

Lee, who has a bachelor's degree in music education from the University of South Carolina and a master's in clinical social work from Florida State, agreed to come to Tallahassee to build a choir of youths, regardless of their ability to sing.

"There are no auditions," Lee said. "It's more than just about singing. Singing is just a tool I use to get them in."

Once a boy, eight to eighteen, joins the choir, he meets three times a week from 2:00 to 5:30 p.m. for study hall. He then goes to choir practice until 8:30. He also receives counseling and learns about social skills, working relationships, reading skills, and ways to resist pressure from peers.

At the onset, success became evident. At the beginning of the school year, fewer boys could boast of success in school than failure. But by the end of the school year, 80–85% were on the academic honor roll. At the same time, their performances achieved incomparable acclaim. Within eight months, the choir took top honors in an international competition.

Today, the choir performs a broad range of songs, from the twenty-nine-page Latin rendition of *Gloria* by Randol Alan Bass to show tunes and R&B. They have added a new song to their repertoire, which they learned for a performance at the White House.

Dana Peck, *Florida State Times*, November 2001

Jack Sams: A Genius Behind IBM PC-DOS Now Shines Light at FSU

In 1998 Jack Sams became the senior licensing manager in the FSU Technology Transfer Office.

Just after the Fourth of July in 1980, Jack Sams flew to Seattle to meet a waifish college dropout named Bill Gates and have a conversation that would change the computer world.

Sams was an IBM software engineer in Boca Raton, part of a maverick team charged with bringing—almost dragging—IBM into the personal-computer market.

The legendarily cautious IBM gave the group just one year to get the job done—but an unprecedented freedom that elated Sams, a $140,000-a-year executive with the soul of a hacker. He would later say in wry understatement, "If it's possible to be an entrepreneur in a corporate environment, then that was the business I was in. I sought those opportunities and was frustrated by most of them. But one succeeded."

He struck a deal with a young kid named Gates.

Knowing that without years of testing, IBM wouldn't develop software to run the PC that would one day be cloned by the industry, Sams' entourage had a single goal: to get someone to provide that pivotal software and operating system and to bear the not-insignificant burden of making sure it worked.

"Bill Gates when I met him was head of a $5-million company, Microsoft, and he didn't have all that much leverage," Sams said from his spartan office in Innovation Park. "But it didn't take long to see that he was a better engineer than my engineer, a better lawyer than my lawyer, and a better programmer than me. And he was only twenty-three."

Soft-spoken, avuncular, and then in his early 50s, Sams struck a deal with Gates (a deal some later blasted, since IBM fell from grace and Gates became the richest man in America). Yet in 1980 IBM got exactly the means-to-an-end it wanted: an operating system that enables the hardware to talk to the software. Though the mercurial Gates didn't have any such thing in hand, he quickly came through.

Sams was among 100,000 IBMers who left the corporation, taking early retirement in 1990 after thirty years. "Tallahassee seemed like a nice place and I thought I'd get an opportunity to teach. Instead I've gotten interested in this innovation business," says Sams, whom you may have seen in "Triumph of the Nerds," a three-hour PBS special about intellectual hotshots.

Can incubation hatch big-time business here? "It's not natural anywhere," he suggests. "Austin was like Tallahassee twenty years ago. Seattle, with Boeing, was just as self-satisfied. Palo Alto was just as provincial in the '50s. All were lovely places dominated by universities or government, oil, airplanes or orchards. The usual problem with the incubation process is that it's conducted primarily with money when the real issue is skill."

Will we know the moment of change? Sams' face becomes mystical, and he grins like a boy: "None of us will ever have met this elephant when it walks in the door, but we just may teach it to dance."

Mary Ann Lindley, *Tallahassee Democrat*, July 14, 1996

"Of all the judges who played a role in this protracted drama, the brightest stars may have been two local judges in Tallahassee. Judges Terry Lewis [1976] and Nikki Clark [1977] conducted their business with dignity and fairness."

NEWSWEEK

Protest in front of the Florida Supreme Court, November 2000

Early on the afternoon of December 9, 2000, a chorus of shouts filled the Tallahassee office of Steel Hector & Davis. It would be almost ten minutes before the rest of the world heard the news: the U.S. Supreme Court had ordered a halt to the recount of contested presidential ballots that was underway four blocks away at the LeRoy Collins Public Library.

Among the exhausted but exhilarated lawyers in the Monroe Street law office that Saturday afternoon were College of Law alumni Donna Blanton, Vicki Weber, John Little, Jon Sjostrom, Betsy Daley, and Beth Maykut. The six were part of the team assigned to represent the Florida Secretary of State's office.

Throughout the five-week post-election drama, scores of FSU law school alumni, faculty, and students were thrust into starring roles. Alumni judges Terry Lewis and Nikki Clark and faculty members Nat Stern and Steve Gey became familiar faces on television broadcasts and front-page newspaper stories around the world.

The law school's location, just two blocks from the state capitol and the Supreme Court, made it almost inevitable that fallout from the historic election would leave an indelible impression.

There were days, in fact, when every article on the front page of the *New York Times* carried a Tallahassee dateline.

The scene in and around the capitol complex assumed the character of a vast movie set. Satellite trucks were lined up as far as the eye could see along South Duval Street and crammed into every loading zone and alley within a quarter-mile radius.

When the curtain came down on the final act at the U.S. Supreme Court the night of December 13, the legions of attorneys who had fought the election's legal wars shared one overwhelming characteristic. "There was a feeling of absolute, total exhaustion," said Broward County Democratic attorney and 1985 FSU Law School graduate Lenny Samuels.

Vicki Weber (1978), whose friendship with Deborah Kearney (1981), general counsel to the Secretary of State, brought Steel Hector & Davis into the case, confirms Samuels' testimony to exhaustion. "The first couple of weeks we were running on adrenaline. After that, it was a grind," she says.

Says John Newton (1977), an attorney for the Democrats, "There was some very good legal work done by both sides under horrible conditions. I think that fact was easy to overlook."

Although the affair put several of the faculty in the national spotlight, none could match the record of Nat Stern. For five weeks his phone rang incessantly. The demands made it impossible, he said, to live anything approaching a normal life.

Gey, who made his arrangement early on with ABC, made dozens of appearances on the network, often in conversation with evening news anchor Peter Jennings.

No alumni received greater publicity—or higher praise—than Judges Clark (1977) and Lewis (1976). "Of all the judges who played a role in this protracted drama," wrote *Newsweek*, "the brightest stars may have been two local judges in Tallahassee. Judges Terry Lewis and Nikki Clark conducted their business with dignity and fairness."

FSU alumni judges not involved in election litigation were drawn into the media glare on Saturday morning, December 9, when they responded to Judge Lewis's order to count contested ballots at the library. Judges Charlie Francis (1972), Tim Harley (1976), and Kathleen Dekker (1977) were among a group that gathered to examine ballots before the U.S. Supreme Court ordered them to stop.

Also at the library that morning was Ion Sancho (1987), Leon County's supervisor of elections.

The final scene of the election drama, played out on a cold, windy night in Washington, D.C., proved to be as bizarre as anything in the previous thirty-five days. The world witnessed the curious spectacle of television correspondents with their noses buried in the unwieldy printed volume of the court's decision. Steve Gey was part of the strange endgame, standing in front of the Florida Supreme Court, wearing an earpiece, straining to hear Peter Jennings in Washington read portions of the final ruling.

Meanwhile, back in Florida, a phalanx of lawyers was about to get its first good night's sleep in more than a month.

David Morrill, *FSU Law,* Spring 2000

Music and song, skywriters and fireworks. Students, alumni, faculty, and staff crowding into Westcott Plaza. Mayors, sheriffs, volunteers in period costumes reenacting the significant events of Florida State University's storied past. Fraternities and sororities hosting exhibit booths. State senators and representatives. Deans and dignitaries. Alumni and friends. They were all there on January 24, 2001, to celebrate the university's 150th birthday.

Frank Murphy, *FSU Times*, February/March 2001

Clockwise from left: FSU's 150th kickoff celebration with current students portraying members of the FSC class of '02; Alan Sundberg and Kitty Hoffman ringing FSCW's dinner bell; Gene Deckerhoff with women in period costumes; Sarah and Josh White in period costumes; Chris Hope lighting torches during FSU's 150th kickoff celebration. Hope, now with the NFL, played defensive safety on the 1999 national championship team.

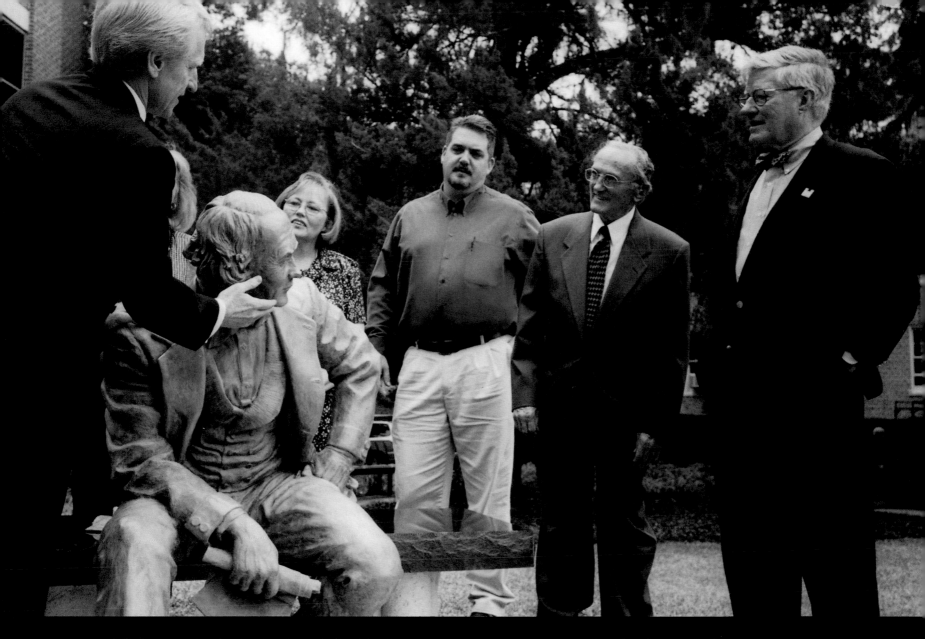

"*Today marks the beginning of Florida State's next 150 years. From this day forward, January 24 will be Heritage Day for FSU, the day when the entire university comes together for the purpose of celebrating our history and accomplishments, the day we look forward to as we celebrate our rich history and welcome the challenges that lie ahead.*"

PRESIDENT TALBOT (SANDY) D'ALEMBERTE

The unveiling of artist Edward Jonas' (L) statue of FSU founding father Francis Eppes, January 24, 2002, at Westcott Plaza. With Eppes descendents present, President D'Alemberte (R) declared the occasion FSU's first annual Heritage Day.

As news of the terrorist attack on the World Trade Center and the Pentagon spread across the FSU campus the morning of September 11, 2001, administrators worked quickly to implement the university's emergency management and communication plans.

After the decision to close all state universities that day was made by Carl Blackwell, chancellor of the Division of Colleges and Universities of the Florida Board of Education, the FSU Police Department took steps to heighten security on campus. Two officers assigned to the Panama City Campus managed the orderly exit of its faculty, staff members, and students and secured its buildings.

President D'Alemberte made the decision to postpone the first meeting of the FSU Board of Trustees until the week of September 17, and by Tuesday night, students had organized an impromptu candlelight vigil on Landis Green.

On Wednesday, President D'Alemberte canceled or postponed all extracurricular activities of a social or celebratory nature.

By Wednesday, the FSU Turkish, Bangladeshi, and Muslim Student associations had made formal statements of outrage and condemnation of the terrorist acts.

On Thursday, roughly 250 students attended a student march from the Oglesby Union to Westcott. Once the marchers had arrived at Westcott, speakers gave messages of patriotism and reassurance and called for prayer.

FSU Media Relations

The long goodbye is over for the Mecca, a Florida State University institution for six decades.

The former restaurant on Copeland Street across from FSU's main gate will be leveled to make way for a new Bill's Bookstore and Art City, which is the Mecca's next-door neighbor and owner.

The move is not sudden: The Mecca closed as a restaurant in 1993, and it was a Bill's Bookstore branch until February of 2002.

But in days gone by, the Mecca was, well, a mecca for art students and psychology professors, sorority girls and hippies, music majors and old grads.

"It was a hangout, and it was wonderful," said Carol Bullock, an FSU academic adviser who worked as a cashier at the Mecca as a student in the early 1970s. "It was a community of its own. A lot of Greeks, a lot of independents, a lot of arty types. If you didn't know the names, you knew the faces."

The Mecca was purchased in the early 1980s by the late Bill Schuessler, the founder of Bill's Bookstore. McNeill, Shuessler's son-in-law, began working at the bookstore in 1982 and became the sole owner in 1999.

A Tallahassee native, McNeill admitted to some nostalgia over the passing of the Mecca.

"The old building was in really bad shape, and it needed to go," McNeill said. "I'm looking forward to the opportunity of a new building."

The Mecca began life as the Spic and Span sandwich shop in the late 1930s. It had a screened-in front porch with a piano that attracted patrons from what was then the Florida State College for Women.

In 1946, World War II veteran Gene Blount and partner Woody Wilson bought the sandwich shop and converted it into a full-service restaurant open from 7 a.m. to 11 p.m. In the late 1960s, Blount's younger brother, Clyde, replaced the late Wilson as a partner.

The restaurant changed its name to the Mecca in the late 1940s, after Blount and Wilson held a contest among the students. The Mecca and the Sweet Shop on Jefferson Street joined the student dining hall as the only places to eat on or close to campus.

"There were only 900 girls [at FSU] our first year. But when all those [former] G.I.s showed up, business just boomed," said Blount, who retired after selling the Mecca to Schuessler. "We had a lot of good years. We met a lot of students, and they were a wonderful clientele. It was a wonderful business."

Gerald Ensley, *Tallahassee Democrat*, March 27, 2002

Artist Ron Yrabedra donated his painting *Seminole Palm* to the 2001 Seven Days of Opening Nights festival. The painting became the festival's official poster. Yrabedra, an FSU alum, has been a professor of art education at Florida A&M for twenty-seven years. In addition to having had many one-man shows, his work is in numerous collections including those of AT&T, North Carolina National Bank, and Barnett Bank.

Margo Bindhart, Chair, Tallahassee: Seven Days of Opening Nights

As Tallahassee celebrates the many expressions of art throughout our community, and as our students benefit each year from exposure to wonderful artists like Claire Bloom, Hal Holbrook, the Boston Pops, Suzanne Farrell Ballet, and Davis Gaines among so many others, we understand more deeply than ever before the importance of the arts in our lives.

> *"Special relationships were formed because of the FSU Florence and London programs. After returning we became, and remain to this day, a sort of subculture of FSU and Tallahassee."*
>
> CECELIA MALONEY (M.A. 1974)

FSU International Programs students, Florence, Italy

International Programs—and Campuses

Florida State University is one of the nation's top-ranked schools for international study. Now offering programs in Africa, Asia, Europe, and Central America, the Office of International Programs (IP) operates year-round campuses in Florence, London, Panama City, and Valencia.

The initial vision of a study center abroad was conceived by Ross Oglesby, dean of students, while escorting the FSU circus through Europe in 1964. Inspired by the city of Florence, Italy, Oglesby suggested that FSU buy a villa and establish a center. After two years of incubation, the Florence Program was born. The London program followed in four years.

English Professor Dr. Conrad Tanzy, later the stateside director of the Florence/London Program, traveled to Florence to set up the center.

In London, Florida State University has offered students a small liberal arts college atmosphere for thirty years. Small classes, American and British teacher-scholars, an historic setting in the heart of the Bloomsbury district—the FSU London Study Center is a benchmark program for study abroad.

According to Jim Pitts, director of International Programs, "Florida State University continues to be a worldwide pacesetter in international education—each year building on our tradition of long leadership to meet today's accelerating, exciting globalism. Through our challenging academic programs, students can study in Italy, England, and Spain; in Russia and the Czech Republic; in Croatia and Vietnam; in France and Greece; in Barbados, Costa Rica, and the Republic of Panama."

One of the many advantages of studying at Florida State is the impressive selection of programs abroad that the university offers. The student who so wishes can, over a four-year period, take classes in Europe, Africa, and Southeast Asia. While this presents a wonderful opportunity for young people, faculty who teach on these programs also profit, even if the pleasure of being in places like Paris or Florence has occasional moments when staying in Tallahassee appears to have been the wiser option.

Take Monday, for example, in Florence when a student did not show up for class. This was not a cause of great concern until the middle of the afternoon when the young woman in question caught up with me outside the FSU Study Center. She was extremely apologetic and explained that on a trip to the island of Elba she ran out of money. Happily for her (!), she ran into three "charming" Italian sailors who assured her they would get her home safely. So she went off with them on a private boat. As I listened to her story, I had a truly special moment. I know few men who can remember feeling their hair turn gray.

But of course the three charming sailors were indeed that. Here the student was. They got her to the mainland, bought her a train ticket for Florence, and sent her on her way.

Everyone expects students to learn a great deal on a program abroad. Whether faculty expect it or not, they have the same experience.

Etruscan and Roman Artifacts

For twenty-five years the site of an ancient Etruscan village has been excavated by student and professional archaeologists led by FSU classics professor Nancy de Grummond, one of the world's leading experts on Etruscan civilization. "The Etruscans are important because they ruled Italy before the Romans," she said. "At Cetamura we have material from the final centuries of their history (300–50 B.C.)."

Of particular interest, de Grummond said, is an artisans' area where there is evidence of weaving, metal-working and the making of ceramics.

More exciting, said de Grummond, "is that we have evidence that they dedicated the kiln to the gods so that they might have success with the labor-intensive, difficult process of making brick and tile."

Cetamura's historical significance stretches into the Roman era as well, she said. "We have excavated the remains of some [Roman] baths with a sophisticated under-floor heating system, dating to the first and second centuries of this era." Included among the relics are Roman board and dice games used to relax while at the baths and artifacts related to grooming and dressing.

Mark Riordan

She's a delightful rags-to-riches story: a woman whose path out of the Florida woods led her to the Florida State College for Women, a career with the Veteran's Administration as a chief dietitian and, with the help of a little prudent investing, a million-dollar donation to FSU's new alumni center.

She credits her mother for her inspiration and her father for her self-confidence: "My mother always said, 'Be somebody.'" Come hog butchering time, her father would "hold the hog while I hit him in the head." With other farm tasks, he would say, "Pearl, you go do it."

Today, the ninety-two-year-old Tyner still farms the acreage around her Laurel Hill home and rides her own tractor. She occasionally journeys to Mississippi where she plays the slots at gambling casinos. But she never forgot where she came from.

"I was a poor girl who worked on a farm," she said in a soft drawl sprinkled with laughs. "We had two mules."

Tyner graduated from high school in 1926 and won a scholarship to FSCW. Higher education was made easier with the help of certain mentors. Tyner's hefty donations to FSU are in tribute to their kindness. "It's the people who were there to help us get an education," she said. "I just came out of the woods. They treated me good."

Among those Tyner remembers most fondly are the school's dietitian, who gave her a job, and her biology teacher.

"I just held them in great esteem," she said. Her only regret is that she never had time for sports.

Following graduation in 1930, Tyner left for Chicago and landed a teaching job. Then, as World War II raged in Europe, she joined the U.S. Army and served in England and France.

The road to wealth began when she worked at the Veteran's Administration. Tyner said she decided to invest some of her wages in the stock market. Then she hung on as the financial roller coaster took off.

At the time of her latest million-dollar gift to FSU, her investments had grown to almost $2 million. So why give away another million, this time toward the creation of the new alumni center which will be named for her?

"I had the money, number one," Tyner said. And number two, she suggested, FSU needs it more than she does: "You stew that money up with hog jowls, but it don't taste like collard greens."

Michelle Hayes, Alumni Association, 2001

Pearl Tyner graduated from high school in 1926 and won a scholarship to FSCW.

My husband went to his office one day and announced that I was going to go back to school to get my master's in English. A friend warned him: "Last woman I knew who went back to school ran off with a poet."

"Oh, Mama," my oldest daughter said, "I hope you're not going to turn into one of those terrible returning women. We just dreaded them in college. They talked and talked in class and put the rest of us to shame by being so overly prepared."

Finally, I got to the first step: an appointment with the chairman of the English Department. He was encouraging, telling me there were lots of returning women. I enrolled, for a class entitled Literary Expression of Popular Culture, and later took creative writing classes. I discovered that writing styles had changed. I tended to over-punctuate. My sentences were all too long, too formal. I didn't tell enough. I tried to be too mysterious.

There were many other things I had to "unlearn." First off, I had to forget my homeroom mother mentality. The only schools I had been in in the past twenty-five years were my three children's. For my classes at FSU I was often the first one there, and if need be I'd gather up loose papers and empty Coke cans and straighten up the rows of desks, even move them into a large circle. On Valentine's Day I brought in candy and heart-shaped napkins. I was shocked to discover that this behavior was never acknowledged and that nobody was particularly friendly. When I mentioned this to my daughter she was appalled. "Mama," she said. "How embarrassing! You're not at a cocktail party. You don't have to speak to everybody that comes along."

I found that I was in a space somewhere in transition. I didn't fit in completely as a student, nor did I in my old life either. Maybe that's why there is no really clear name for us. We were returning women, nontraditional students. We were even known as chronologically challenged students.

There is value in not completely fitting in anywhere. I saw how judgmental I had been now that I was being judged. Old and loyal friends cheered me on, read my stories, and respected the time I needed for work. Some friends were lost along the way, but I made new ones. My friends, old and new, came to supper and celebrated with me when my first story was accepted for publication.

I found professors who encouraged me to talk and write about my experiences and who gave unstintingly of their time; I also learned to respect the work of teachers I didn't personally care for.

Now that I have the degree I went back to school to earn, have had more stories published, and am working on a novel, I realize that the name I like best for what I was is simply "student." It states the fact. It does not require excuses or explanations of why it took us so long to get back. It puts the burden squarely on ourselves.

Gus Stavros was the benefactor responsible for the Gus. A. Stavros Center for Free Enterprise and Economic Education. President emeritus Bernard Sliger is the director.

SESQUICENTENNIAL FSU

Jerome Stern: University

Jerry Stern was a professor of English at FSU until his death in 1996. His monologues, including the one below, were heard regularly on National Public Radio.

I was in the office reading term papers, chair tilted back, my feet propped against the edge of the desk. A knock at the door, and a blond, kind of heavy guy, early thirties, looking vaguely familiar, sticks his head in, smiles big, and says, "Hey, just thought I'd drop by and say hello."

It was a student whom I hadn't seen in, I don't know, seven years or more, and when he said his name I remembered his quick mind and the class he was in, and some of the other people he hung out with.

He tells me what he's been doing—went to the Coast with a friend, got bit parts in cheapo horror movies, managed a fern bar; lived in Mexico, worked on a coastal steamer; got deadly ill, finally went to law school, married now with a kid.

And I thought, Here this person has been doing all this and he finds his teacher in the same position he left him seven years ago, feet on the desk, reading term papers.

I thought about what that might mean and what he might be thinking, and should I worry about it? Was I one of those characters who seem never to live, who work forty years for the firm, never looking past their green eyeshades?

What should I do? Get a ticket to Katmandu? Buy a monster truck? And then I thought, no, that my obligation was not to become a Zen Buddhist in Colorado, then do stand-up-comedy in New Jersey, get interested in welding, and finally take up large-scale sculpture out of wrecked car chassis. And not to have tempestuous relationships with a historic succession of people who would break tables, wreck cars, have to be dried or bailed out at frequent intervals.

Perhaps it was my calling to do what I love—to read, write, talk about what I learned, think up theories to explain things, and keep my feet on the desk. You return to your college town; the stores you shopped in have vanished utterly, the bars you drank in have different names, the restaurants you ate in are law offices, and the houses you rented have been bulldozed.

The university itself, though, should be the one place where the trees are as green as you remember, the buildings standing just where you left them; the halls should be beige, the posters should be tattered, the classrooms vaguely grimy. The students scraggly, scruffy, smooth or sleek, but doing the same things, hanging out, talking on the steps, yelling from cars.

And when you come to a familiar office door you should be able to knock, and have someone look up at you from a desk littered with what looks like what was on it when you left several lifetimes ago, and that person should tilt his head back and say hello in that voice that meant something to you back then.

And you can feel the pleasure that might come from staying in one place to think, to learn, to pass on what meant something to you a long time ago, and what you came back to find.

Jerome Stern, *Radios: Short Takes on Life and Culture*, W.W. Norton, 1997

Opposite:
Jerry Stern,
Professor of English,
in his office at FSU,1984

FSU Film School student projects

Jawole Willa Jo Zollar is a dance professor and creator and member of the Urban Bush Women, an acclaimed New York–based dance troupe. In 1999 she won FSU's Dr. Martin Luther King, Jr., Distinguished Service Award.

Top: Lawrence G. Abele, FSU Provost and Vice- President for Academic Affairs, formerly chairperson of the Department of Biological Science (1983–91) and dean of the College of Arts and Sciences (1991–94)

Below: Winston Scott, an FSU ODK Grad Made Good, served as an astronaut for NASA, National Aeronautics and Space Administration, from 1992 to 1998. He came to FSU as associate vice-president for student affairs in 1999. He has taught electrical engineering at both Florida Community College and Florida A&M University.

Daniel Cook (class of 2001)

I will never forget the telephone conversation I had with an admissions officer one late night. I was a senior in high school and called the officer back at eight p.m. He was working late and answered my call. I was shocked to hear that FSU would probably not accept me for the fall semester, but that I would probably be allowed to attend the university if I came for summer. We talked for about half an hour, and I accepted the summer term because I was going to do whatever it took to be a Seminole.

I spent four years dedicating my time to FSU, the community, and my fellow Seminoles. I had the opportunity to serve as a host in the president's skybox during football games and was myself a guest when selected for the 2000 homecoming court.

I served the Student Alumni Association as vice-president and the Seminole Leadership Experience as chairman and co-chairman.

FSU said thank you to me when I was selected to be in the Senior Wall of Fame in spring 2001, but it is I that am still finding new ways to say thank you to FSU.

John Carnaghi, Vice-President for Administrative Affairs

My ten years of service to Florida State make me a relative newcomer. However, my time here has been one of excitement, invigoration, and challenge that I never experienced in my twenty-three years at a Big Ten school.

Florida State has emerged from being a reasonably respected university to one of the most dynamic institutions of higher education in America. There are many reasons for this having happened but much of the impetus was due to one man's leadership and vision, namely that of Sandy D'Alemberte.

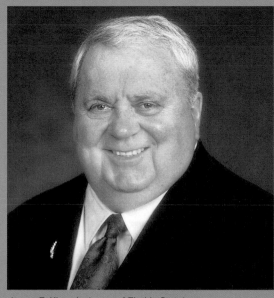

John Thrasher (class of 1965, J.D. 1972) was the 1999–2000 speaker of the House of Representatives. He is currently a member of the law firm Smith, Hulsey & Busey in Jacksonville, president of Southern Strategy Group, and Chairman of the FSU Board of Trustees.

James E. King, Jr., is one of Florida State's more prominent alumni, having served in the Florida Legislature since 1986. Elected first to the House of Representatives and subsequently to the Senate, Senator King has been a tremendous supporter of FSU, its academics and athletics, on both sides of the aisle.

Board of Trustees

The 2001 Legislature passed significant reforms to the education delivery system of Florida for the purpose of creating a seamless education experience for students enrolled in the K-20 system. As a result, the legislation abolished the Florida Board of Regents and transfered its functions and duties to the newly created Florida Board of Education effective on July 1, 2001.

The board members are Erich Bloch, Washington D.C.; Emily Fleming Duda,Oviedo; David Ford, Rosemount; Dr. Jessie Furlow, Quincy; William Haggard, Coral Gables; Manny Garcia, Winter Springs; Lee Hinkle, Tallahassee; Harold Knowles, Tallahassee; Dr. J. Stanley Marshall, Tallahassee; Dr. E. Ann McGee, Winter Springs; John Thrasher, Orange Park; Steven J. Uhlfelder, Tallahassee; and Michelle T. Pletch, Winter Park, elected president by the FSU student body.

The fall 2001 enrollment totaled 35,462 students from all 50 states and over 139 countries. The breakdown by class included 6,815 freshmen, 5,384 sophomores, 7,447 juniors, 7,479 seniors, 696 law students, 2,020 special students, and 5,621 graduate students. Of the student body, 43.57% were men, 56.43% women. The faculty totaled 1,956.

FUTURE SEMINOLES

Sydney Cook

Beverly Spencer, Florida House of Representatives, 1976–1988; Florida Assistant Secretary of State, 1988–1992; Vice-President, University Relations, FSU; B.A.1962

Beverly Burnsed Spencer, Vice-President, University Relations

When I think of the word *history* in relation to Florida State University, it takes on a special meaning. To me it means those things worth remembering, a long and happy relationship that only got better with time. FSU was my alma mater and FSU will be the place I retire from. It is this university that has shaped who I am. All of you have your own memories, your own history. It doesn't matter if your thoughts are of FSCW or Florida State University. Many of you have adopted FSU because you have come to know the campus while attending lectures, plays, concerts, or sporting events. Florida State embraces you all; we are glad you have shared in the 150th anniversary celebration.

And remember, the best is yet to come. Future Seminoles are born every day.

From top left, L to R: Joseph Michael Carbonara; Sarah Boland; Bobby Celander; Cannon Randle; Mary Lanier Odom; Lauren Lee Soriano; Dezmond Barkley; Joya Earnest; Brandon Johnson; Juliana Atwell; Alex and Gaby Suarez; Rachael, Seth and Abigail Agwunobi; Shannon Nicole Pate; Gatlin Blake Miller; Geena Leigh Bruno; Madeline Feiock; Kira Smith; Katie and Colin Kliner

Some Grads at a Glance From the Alumni Association

Caroline Alexander, author, FSU's first Rhodes scholar, B.A. 1976

Martha Bedell Alexander, NC State Representative, B.S. 1961

Douglas J. Allen, Cdr., U.S.D.A.O., ODK Grad Made Good, B.S. 1976

Michael E. Allen, Judge, 1st District Court of Appeal, B.S. 1971

James H. Ammons, Provost, Florida A&M University, M.S.P. 1975, Ph.D. 1971

John Antoon, Judge, U.S. District Court, J.D. 1971

Reubin Askew, former Governor of Florida, ODK Grad Made Good, B.S. 1951

Paul Azinger, golf pro, PGA, attendee 1983

Alan Ball, Oscar-winning screen writer, *American Beauty*, attendee 1980

Kim Batten, FSU faculty, U.S. Olympic medalist, track and field, 2000, B.S. 1983

Allan G. Bense, Florida House of Representatives, B.A. 1972, M.A. 1974

Michael Berenbaum, Shoah Foundation, ODK Grad Made Good, Ph.D. 1975

Fred Biletnikoff, Coach, Orlando Raiders, attendee 1965

Harry R. Blieden, ODK Grad Made Good, Ph.D. 1962

Allen Boyd, Jr., U.S. House of Representatives, B.S. 1969

John Bradley, actor, *Robinhood*, B.A. 1981

Derrick Brooks, pro football, Tampa Bay Bucs, B.S. 1994, M.S. 1999

Frank D. Brown, President, Columbus State University, Ph.D. 1974

Norma E. Brown, Major General, ODK Grad Made Good, B.S. 1949

Ed Browning, Judge, Florida 1st District Court of Appeal, B.S. 1961

David B. Burks, President, Harding University, Ph.D. 1974

Antonio J. Busalacchi, Jr., University of Maryland/Earth System Science Interdisciplinary Center, formerly with NASA, ODK Grad Made Good, B.S. 1977, M.S. 1980, Ph.D. 1982

LeRoy Butler, pro football, Green Bay Packers, attendee 1990

Clifton Campbell, Executive Producer, *Sea Quest DSV, Profiler*, B.F.A. 1979

Joseph Camps, M.D., physician, B.S. 1979

Raoul G. Cantero, III, Judge, Florida Supreme Court, B.S. 1982

Virginia S. Carr, Georgia State University, ODK Grad Made Good, BA 1951, Ph.D. 1969

Sam Cassell, pro basketball, Milwaukee Bucks, attendee 1993

Chip Chalmers, Director/Producer, *Beverly Hills 90210, Melrose Place*, ODK Grad Made Good, B.F.A. 1976

W.D. Childers, former U.S. Senator, B.S. 1955

Warren H. Cobb, Judge, 5th District Court of Appeal, B.S. 1955

Rita Coolidge, singer, actress, B.A 1967

Lee Corso, ESPN commentator, B.S. 1957, M.S. 1958

Raymond Cottrell, M.D., physician, B.S. 1969

Dave Cowans, NBA Basketball Hall of Fame, formerly with Charlotte Hornets, B.S.W. 1971

Larry Crow, VP and Senior Science Advisor, IIT Research Institute, ODK Grad Made Good, B.S. 1966, M.S. 1967, Ph.D. 1971

Thomas E. Culligan, Executive VP, Business Development, President, Raytheon International, Inc., ODK Grad Made Good, B.A. 1973, M.P.A. 1977

William O. Cullom, Greater Miami Chamber of Commerce, ODK Grad Made Good, B.S. 1958

Charles J. Cunningham, Jr., Lt. General (ret.), SHAPE Intel, ODK Grad Made Good, B.S. 1957

John D'Aquino, actor, *Seaquest, Third Rock from the Sun, Melrose Place, Silk Stalkings*, attendee 1981

Marguerite Davis, Judge, 1st District Court of Appeal, J.D. 1971

Brendon Dedekind, South Africa Olympic swim team, 2000, B.S. 1999

Arnold T. Diaz, ABC News, *20/20*, ODK Grad Made Good, B.A. 1971

J.D. Drew, pro baseball, St. Louis Cardinals, attendee 1998

Warrick Dunn, pro football, Tampa Bay Buccaneers, B.S. 1997

Jacqueline Dupont, A.O. Atwater Award winner, retired U.S. Department of Agriculture, ODK Grad Made Good, B.S. 1955, Ph.D. 1962

Jacquelyn Dupont-Walker, President, Ward Economic Development, B.S. 1966

Sylvia Earle, oceanographer/deep ocean engineering, ODK Grad Made Good, B.S. 1955

Mark S. Ellis, formerly with International Bar Association, ODK Grad Made Good, B.A. 1979, J.D. 1974

Richard W. Ervin, III, Judge, 1st District Court of Appeal, B.A. 1957

Frank Fain, M.D., physician, B.A. 1957

Robert L. Floyd, II, Brig. General, U.S. Navy, B.A. 1969

Neil Frank, meteorologist, ODK Grad Made Good, M.S. 1959, Ph.D. 1970

Corey Fuller, pro football, Cleveland Browns, B.S. 1996

Davis Gaines, actor, *Phantom of the Opera*, ODK Grad Made Good, B.A. 1976

Jane Geddes, golf pro, LPGA, attendee 1982

Steven Geller, Florida House of Representatives, B.A. 1979, J.D. 1982

William H. Ginn, Jr., Lt. General, ODK Grad Made Good, B.A. 1958

Parris Glendening, Governor of Maryland, B.S. 1964, M.A. 1965, Ph.D. 1967

W. Tom Gould, Chairman & CEO (ret.), Younkers, B.S. 1969

Bud Grace, political cartoonist, ODK Grad Made Good, B.S. 1965, Ph.D. 1971

Arnold Greenfield, attorney (ret.), Managing Director, Lehman Brothers, B.S. 1958

Carolyn S. Griner, NASA, ODK Grad Made Good, B.S. 1967

Thomas M. Hall, ODK Grad Made Good, B.M. 1964, M.M. 1966

Barbara Harris, ODK Grad Made Good, Editor, *Shape Magazine*, B.S. 1978

Charles (Chris) Hart, IV, Florida Senate, B.S. 1991

Robert Hebert, President, McNeese State University, M.A. 1961, Ph.D. 1966

Kitty Blood Hoffman, former FSU administrator, Professor of Chemistry Emerita, B.S. 1936

Gordon Holder, Vice-Admiral, U.S. Navy, B.M.E. 1968

Tara Dawn Holland (Christensen), former Miss America (1997), B.M.E. 1994

Robert (Bob) Holton, developer of Taxol, a cancer fighting drug, M.S. 1970, Ph.D. 1971

Glenda Briscoe Hope, Rev., San Francisco Network Ministries, B.A. 1958

Jim Horne, Florida Senate, B.S. 1980

Mallory Horne, former Florida Senate President and House of Representatives Speaker, attendee 1946–47

Traylor Howard, Actress, B.S. 1989

Jennifer Howse, President, March of Dimes, ODK Grad Made Good, B.A. 1966, M.A.1968, Ph.D. 1973

Janice Huff, meteorologist, NBC *Today Show*, B.S. 1982

Marvalene Hughes, President, California State University, Stanislaus, Turlock, Ca., Ph.D. 1969

Paul Jadin, Mayor, City of Green Bay, Wisconsin, M.S.P. 1979

James Joanos, Judge, 1st District Court of Appeal, B.S. 1956

Brad Johnson, quarterback, Washington Redskins, B.S. 1992

James (Jim) R. Jorgenson, Judge, 3rd District Court of Appeal, B.S. 1966, J.D. 1968

Lynda Keever, Publisher, *Florida Trend Magazine*, B.A. 1969

William Kerr, Msgr., President, Laroche College, ODK Grad Made Good, M.A. 1973, Ph.D. 1975

Carl M. Kuttler, Jr., President, St. Petersburg Jr. College, B.S. 1962

Christine Lahti, actress, attendee 1976

Tony LaRussa, Manager, St. Louis Cardinals, J.D. 1978

Al Lawson, Florida House of Representatives, B.A. 1973

Joseph Lewis, Jr., Judge,1st District Court of Appeal, J.D. 1977

Judy P. Lotas, ODK Grad Made Good, B.A. 1964

Mary Anne Loughlin, news anchor, *News 12*, Tallahassee, ODK Grad Made Good, B.S. 1977

E. Ann McGee, President, Seminole Community College, B.A. 1970, M.A. 1970

John McKay, President, Florida Senate, B.W. 1971

Scott Maddox, Mayor, Tallahassee, B.S. 1989, J.D. 1994

Doug Marlette, Pulitzer Prize–winning cartoonist, ODK Grad Made Good, B.S. 1971

Mel Martinez, Chairman, Orange County, Florida; appointed U.S. Secretary of Housing and Urban Development, 2001; B.A. 1969, J.D. 1973

James L. Massey, ODK Grad Made Good, B.S. 1965

DeLane Matthews, actress, *Dave's World*, B.F.A. 1983

Doug Mientkiewicz, pro baseball, U.S. Olympics 2000, attendee 1996

Paul D. Miller, Admiral (ret.), U.S. Navy, CEO/Chairman, Alliant Techsystems, ODK Grad Made Good, B.S. 1963

Charles E. Miner, Jr., Judge, 1st District Court of Appeal, B.S. 1955

Kenneth Minihan, Lt. General, National Security Agency, ODK Grad Made Good, B.A. 1966

Richard E. Mitchell, Florida House of Representatives, B.S. 1979

Stephen Montague, pianist/composer/ orchestra musician, B.M. 1965, M.M. 1967

Herb P. Morgan, former member Florida House of Representatives; Executive VP, Florida Association of Insurance and Financial Advisors; ODK Grad Made Good; B.S. 1966

Bryan Norcross, meteorologist, WFOR-TV, Miami, B.S. 1972, M.S. 1980

Carolyn O'Neil, anchor, CNN, ODK Grad Made Good, B.S. 1976

Phil Padovano, Judge, 1st District Court of Appeal, B.S. 1969

Edmund Pankau, Investigator/CEO, Pankau Consulting, B.S. 1972

Mike Pate, Publisher, *Tallahassee Democrat*, B.S. 1968

Brett Petersen, South Africa Olympic Swim Team, 2000, current student

Earl W. Peterson, Jr., Judge, 5th District Court of Appeal, B.S. 1957

Michael Piontek, actor, *Phantom of the Opera, Beauty and the Beast,* B.S. 1981, M.F.A. 1985

Henry Polic, actor, ODK Grad Made Good, B.A 1967, M.A. 1969

Ricky Polston, Judge,1st District Court of Appeal, B.S. 1977, J.D. 1986

Dallas Raines, meteorologist, KABC/TV, California State University, Northridge, B.S. 1976

Gabrielle Reece, pro volleyball, former model/talk show host, attendee 1990

Clyda Stokes Rent, President, Mississippi University for Women, ODK Grad Made Good, B.A .1964, M.S. 1966, Ph.D. 1968

Burt Reynolds, actor, attendee 1954–57, honorary doctorate 1981

Emilie Richards, romance novelist, B.A. 1970

Curtis Richardson, Florida House of Representatives 2001, B.S. 1978, M.S. 1983

Victor Rivers, actor, *Zorro, Amistad*, B.S. 1977

Marcus Roberts, jazz musician, attendee 1980s

C. Paul Robinson, Director, Sandia National Labs, ODK Grad Made Good, Ph.D. 1967

Peter Romero, Assistant U.S. Secretary of State for Inter-American Affairs, B.S. 1971, M.A. 1972

Stephen J. Rothman, Pennsylvania State University, ODK Grad Made Good, B.S. 1972, M.F.A. 1974

Francisco J. Sanchez, Assistant Secretary for Aviation, U.S. Department of Transportation, B.A. 1982, J.D. 1986

Deion Sanders, pro football, Washington Redskins, attendee 1988

Winston Scott, FSU administration, astronaut, ODK Grad Made Good, B.M.E. 1972

Steven Sears, Executive Producer, *Xena-Warrior Princess, Raven*, B.A. 1980

Ron Sellers, College Football Hall of Fame, B.S. 1969

Randy Ser, Emmy Award–winning art director, B.A. 1975, M.F.A. 1977

Jeff Shaara, author, *Gods and Generals, The Last Full Measure*, B.S. 1974

Mike Sheridan, Brig. General (ret.), Rose Packing Company, ODK Grad Made Good, B.S. 1956

Sonny Shroyer, actor, *Dukes of Hazzard*, attendee 1954

Betty L. Siegel, President, Kennesaw State University, ODK Grad Made Good, Ph.D. 1961

Richard Simmons, entertainer/fitness personality, B.A. 1970

Ron Simmons, pro wrestler, entertainer, attendee 1979

Christopher L. Smith, Florida House of Representatives, J.D. 1995

C. David Smith, M.D., physician, B.S. 1976

Jim Smith, Secretary of State, former Florida Attorney General, ODK Grad Made Good, B.S. 1962

Ken Sorensen, Florida House of Representatives, M.A. 1989

Tonea Stewart, actress, *Heat of the Night, A Time to Kill, Walker Texas Ranger*, Alabama State University Professor, Ph.D. 1989

Janet Stoner, Texaco executive, ODK Grad Made Good, B.S. 1970, MS 1972

F. William Summers, Director, FSU University Library, professor and former dean FSU, former State Librarian of Florida, B.A. 1955

Bob Sura, pro basketball, Golden Gate Warriors, attendee 1994

Cynthia J. Taylor, ODK Grad Made Good, B.S. 1974, M.S. 1975

R. Eugene Taylor, President, Bank of America, Consumer and Commercial Banking, B.S. 1969

Norm Thagard, M.D., astronaut, FSU faculty, ODK Grad Made Good, B.S. 1965, M.S. 1966

James H. Thompson, former Speaker, Florida House of Representatives, D.A. 1955, J.D. 1969

John Thrasher, FSU Board of Trustees, former Speaker, Florida House of Representatives, B.S. 1965, J.D. 1972

James B. Tippin, Jr., ODK Grad Made Good, B.S. 1950

Hansel Tookes, II, President and CEO, Raytheon Aircraft, B.S. 1969

H. James Towey, CEO, Aging with Dignity, former head of Florida HRS, B.S. 1978, J.D. 1981

Willis N. Tyrrell, Jr., geologist, ODK Grad Made Good, B.S. 1952

Balint Vazsonyi, pianist, M.M. 1960

J. Alex Villalobos, Florida House of Representatives, J.D. 1988

Claudia Waite, soprano, M.M. 1996

Charlie Ward, football Heisman Trophy winner, pro basketball, New York Knicks, B.S. 1993

Leslie Waters, Florida House of Representatives, B.S. 1969, M.S. 1970

Charlotte West, ODK Grad Made Good, B.S. 1954

T.K. Wetherell, former Speaker, Florida House of Representatives, former President, Tallahassee Community College; B.S. 1967, M.S. 1968, Ph.D. 1974

Bailey White, author, commentator, National Public Radio; teacher, Thomas County, Ga.; ODK Grad Made Good, B.S. 1973

Douglas M. Windham, SUNY-Albany University, ODK Grad Made Good, B.A. 1964, M.A. 1967, Ph.D. 1969

Mark S. Wrighton, Chancellor, Washington University, ODK Grad Made Good, B.S. 1969

Suzan L. Zeder, University of Texas, Theatre for Youth Chair, ODK Grad Made Good, Ph.D. 1978

Linda Zoghby, soprano, opera artist, ODK Grad Made Good, B.M. 1971, M.M. 1974

Jawole Willa Jo Zollar, founder, award-winning *Urban Bush Women* dance troupe, New York, faculty FSU, ODK Grad Made Good, M.F.A. 1979

Ellen Taafe Zwilich, Pulitzer Prize winner in music, ODK Grad Made Good, B.M. 1960, M.M. 1962

University & Faculty Facts From *FSU Fact Book 2001–2002*

ROBERT O. LAWTON DISTINGUISHED PROFESSORS

The Robert O. Lawton Distinguished Professor award is the highest honor faculty can bestow on a colleague. First presented in 1957–58 the award was known as the Distinguished Professor award until 1981 when it was renamed in honor of the late vice-president for academic affairs Robert O. Lawton. At that time past recipients also were designated Lawton Distinguished Professors.

1957–58
William Hudson Rogers, English

1958–59
Marian Doris Irish, Government

1959–60
Anna Forbes Liddell, Philosophy

1960–61
Ernest Max Grunwald, Chemistry

1961–62
Wiley Lee Housewright, Music

1962–63
Michael Kasha, Chemistry

1963–64
Dorothy Lois Breen Hoffman, Modern Languages

1964–65
Carlisle Floyd, Jr., Music

1965–66
Betty Monaghan Watts, Food and Nutrition

1966–67
Raymond K. Sheline, Chemistry

1967–68
Gregory R. Choppin, Chemistry

1968–69
Eugene D. Nichols, Mathematics Education

1969–70
Earl Frieden, Chemistry

1970–71
Ralph Allan Bradley, Statistics

1971–72
Lloyd Mumbauer Beidler, Biological Science

1972–73
Kellogg Wesley Hunt, English

1973–74
I. Richard Savage, Statistics

1974–75
Daniel Ralph Kenshalo, Psychology

1975–76
Richard Gordon Fallon, Theatre

1976–77
Elena Nikolaidi, Music

1977–78
Richard L. Rubenstein, Religion

1978–79
Seymour L. Hess, Meteorology

1979–80
George M. Harper, English

1980–81
Harry M. Walborsky, Chemistry

1981–82
Robert Gilmer, Mathematics

1982–83
Robert M. Gagne, Educational Research, Development, and Foundations

1983–84
J. Herbert Taylor, Biological Science

1984–85
Leo Mandelkern, Chemistry
Frank Proschan, Statistics

1985–86
T.N. Krishnamurti, Meteorology

1986–87
Daniel Simberloff, Biological Science

1987–88
Werner Herz, Chemistry

1988–89
Clifford K. Madsen, Music

1989–90
Richard L. Greaves, History

1990–91
Donald Robson, Physics
Nancy Smith Fichter, Dance

1991–92
E. Imre Friedmann, Biological Science

1992–93
James C. Smith, Psychology

1993–94
Jayaram Sethuraman, Statistics

1994–95
Kurt G. Hofer, Biological Science

1995–96
Janet G. Burroway, English

1996–97
Joseph Travis, Biological Science

1997–98
DeWitt Sumners, Mathematics

1998–99
Myles Hollander, Statistics

1999–00
James J. O'Brien, Meteorology and Oceanography

2000–01
Christopher K.W. Tam, Mathematics

2001–02
Nancy H. Marcus, Oceanography

NATIONAL ACADEMY OF SCIENCES

Ten faculty members have been elected members of the National Academy of Sciences. The seven current or retired are:

Louis N. Howard, Mathematics (retired in 1995)

Michael Kasha, Chemistry

Donald L. Casper, Biological Science

J. Robert Schrieffer, Physics

Zachary Fisk, Physics

Melvin E. Stern, Oceanography

Lloyd M. Biedler, Biological Science (retired in 1993)

AMERICAN ACADEMY OF ARTS AND SCIENCES

Michael Kasha, Chemistry

Louis N. Howard, Mathematics (retired in 1995)

Lloyd M. Beidler, Biological Science (retired in 1993)

Donald L. Casper, Biological Science

NOBEL LAUREATES

A total of five Nobel Laureates have served on staff at Florida State University.

Konrad E. Bloch, Human Sciences

James M. Buchanan, Economics

Robert Sanderson Mulliken, Chemical Physics

Paul A.M. Dirac, Physics

J. Robert Schrieffer, Physics (currently on staff)

SCHOOLS AND COLLEGES

Florida State University comprises seventeen active schools and colleges, plus Graduate Studies. Opinions differ as to the exact dates some schools and colleges were officially founded. The following represents the best estimate available.

College of Arts and Sciences, 1905

College of Education, 1905

College of Human Sciences, 1918

School of Music, 1921

School of Information Studies, 1947

Graduate Studies, 1947

School of Social Work, 1949

College of Business, 1950

School of Nursing, 1950

School of Public Administration, 1949 (discontinued 1959)

School of Journalism, 1950 (discontinued 1959)

School of Engineering Science, 1963 (discontinued 1972)

College of Law, 1966

School of Criminology and Criminal Justice, 1973

College of Social Sciences, 1973

College of Communication, 1973

School of Theatre, 1973

School of Visual Arts and Dance, 1973

FAMU/FSU College of Engineering, 1981

School of Motion Picture, Television and Recording Arts, 1988

College of Medicine, 2001

DR. MARTIN LUTHER KING, JR., DISTINGUISHED SERVICE AWARD

The award honors a faculty member for outstanding service in keeping with the principles and ideals of the late civil rights leader.

1986 **William R. Jones**, Black Studies

1987 **Na'im Akbar**, Psychology

1988 **David L. Ammerman**, History

1989 **Douglas G. St. Angelo**, Political Science
Maxine D. Jones, History

1990 **Melvin T. Stith**, Marketing

1991 **Joe M. Richardson**, History

1992 **Sandra Rackley**, Associate Dean, Undergraduate Studies

1993 **Freddie Groomes**, Director, University Human Resources

1994 **R. Bruce Bickley, Jr.**, English

1995 **Fred Seamon**, Public Administration

1996 **Andre J. Thomas**, Music

1997 **Sheila Ortiz-Taylor**, English

1998 **Joy M. Bowen**, Executive Assistant, Student Affairs

1999 **Jawole Willa Jo Zollar**, Dance

2000 **Edward Love**, Sculptor

2001 **Billy R. Close**, Criminology and Criminal Justice

2002 **Jenice Rankins**, Nutrition, Food, and Exercise Sciences

HONORARY DEGREES AWARDED AND FIELDS OF DISTINCTION

1912 **Rowena Longmire**, Education

1935 **Ruth Bryan Owen Rhode**, Public Service

1950 **Henri Bonnet**, International Affairs

1950 **Mark Frederick Boyd**, Medicine

1952 **Wouter Bleeker**, Science

1955 **William Morrison Robinson, Jr.**, History

1956 **Millard Fillmore Caldwell**, Public Service
LeRoy Collins, Public Service
William George Dodd, Education
Spessard Lindsey Holland, Public Service
Philip Wylie, Literature

1957 **Doak Sheridan Campbell**, Education
Ernst von Dohnányi, Music
George A. Smathers, Public Service

1959 **J. Velma Keen**, Business

1960 **Cyril O. Houle**, Education

1961 **Glen T. Seaborg**, Science
Vivian Ahlsweh Williams, Literature

1962 **Leonard J. Brass**, Science
Thomas B. Swann, Business/Public Service

1963 **Pablo Casals**, Music
Luther H. Hodges, Public Service/Business
Karl Zerbe, Art

1964 **Cecil Farris Bryant**, Public Service
Edwin A. Menninger, Science
Dorothy Barclay Thompson, Journalism

1965 **Arthur Statan Adams**, Science/Public Service/Education
J. J. Daniel, Law/Business
Robert J. Van de Graaff, Science

1968 **Michael E. DeBakey**, Medicine
Lamar Dodd, Art/Education
Robert L. Shaw, Music

1969 **Lucius D. Battle**, Public Service
Andres Segovia, Music

1970 **Alan S. Boyd**, Public Service
Audrey Wood Liebling, Literature/Letter
Gregor Piatigorsky, Music
Nelson Poynter, Public Service
Paul M. Rudolph, Architecture

1971 **Ed V. Komarek**, Science

1972 **Wilbur J. Cohen**, Education
John Mackay Shaw, Poetry

1973 **Karl Dietrich Bracher**, History
William D. McElroy, Science
Allen Morris, Public Service
Julia V. Morton, Science

1975 **Philip Handler**, Science
Helen Hayes MacArthur, Theatre
King Hussein I (Hashemite-Jordan), Public Service

1976 **Chester H. Ferguson**, Education/Public Service
Stephen C. O'Connell, Education/Law

1977 **Mae Knight Clark**, Education
Lee Strasberg, Theatre
Herbert Spencer Zim, Science/Education

1978 **Lillian Gordy Carter**, Public Service
Michael Butler Yeats, International Affairs
William H. Werkmeister, Philosophy

1979 **Rev. Charles K. Steele, Sr.**, Public Service
William Styron, Literature

1980 **B. K. Roberts**, Public Service/Law

1981 **Burt Reynolds**, Theatre

1982 **Roger L. Stevens**, Theatre

1983 **Ricardo De La Espriella**, Public Service
Beth Walton Moor, Public Service
William C. Norris, Business/Public Service

1984 **Rafael Caldera**, Public Service/Education;
John P. McGovern, Medicine

1985 **Claude Pepper**, Public Service

1986 **Don Fuqua**, Science
Daisy Parker Flory, Public Service
Joseph Papp, Theatre

1988 **Reubin Askew**, Public Service
Toshiaki Ogasawara, Public Service

1989 **George Langford**, Business/Public Service
G. William Miller, Finance/Public Service

1990 **D. Burke Kibler**, Business/Public Service

1991 **Gunther Schuller**, Music
Gus A. Stavros, Business/Public Service
Robert Edward Turner III, Business/Public Service
Marguerite Neel Williams, Public Service
Ada Belle Winthrop-King, Modern Languages

1992 **Louise Ireland Humphrey**, Public Service
Oscar Arias Sanchez, Public Service

1993 **Walter Lanier (Red) Barber**, Public Broadcasting
D. Allan Bromley, Public Service

1994 **Betty Mae Jumper**, Public Service
Simon Ostrach, Space Science/Mechanical Engineering

1995 **Rosa L. Parks**, Civil Rights
C. DuBose Ausley, Public Service

1996 **William R. Mote**, Marine Science;
Sir James Lighthill, Mathematics

1997 **Russell V. Ewald**, Public Service
Louis J. Hector, Law
Ben Weider, Public Service
James M. Moran, Business
Richard W. Ervin, Law
Charles B. Reed, Education

1998 **Rod M. Brim, Sr.**, Business
John Paul Stevens, Law
Godfrey Smith, Business

1999 **Mart Pierson Hill**, Public Service
Carl A. DeSantis, Business
Thomas F. Petway III, Business

2000 **James C. Smith**, Public Service

2001 **Ann Reinking,** Theatre
Reid B. Hughes, Business/Public Service

2002 **Charlotte Edwards Maguire**, Medicine

INDEX

FSU